Untwisting Scriptures

THAT WERE USED TO TIE YOU UP, GAG
YOU, AND TANGLE YOUR MIND

BOOK 2
PATRIARCHY AND AUTHORITY

Rebecca Davis

Pennycress Publishing

Greenville, South Carolina

Copyright © 2021 Rebecca Davis.

All rights reserved. No part of this publication may be reproduced, distributed or transmitted in any form or by any means, including photocopying, recording, or other electronic or mechanical methods, without the prior written permission of the publisher, except in the case of brief quotations embodied in critical reviews and certain other noncommercial uses permitted by copyright law.

For permission requests and quantity discounts, write to the author, Rebecca Davis, via the website www.heresthejoy.com.

All Scripture quotations, unless otherwise noted, are from the Holy Bible, English Standard Version® (ESV®), copyright © 2001 by Crossway, a publishing ministry of Good News Publishers. Used by permission. All rights reserved.

Scriptures marked KJV are from The Holy Bible, King James Version.

Scriptures marked NIV are from The Holy Bible, New International Version®, copyright © 1973, 1978, 1984, 2011 by Biblica, Inc.™ Used by permission. All rights reserved worldwide.

Scriptures marked AMP are from the Amplified® Bible, copyright © 2015 by The Lockman Foundation. Used by permission.

Cover photo by Stephanie Council
Cover design by Tim Davis

Untwisting Scriptures that were used to tie you up, gag you, and tangle your mind: Book 2 Patriarchy and Authority / Rebecca Davis. —first edition.

ISBN 9780998943558

*Dedicated to the wonderful survivors
of cults and cult-like churches,
who still long to know the true Jesus.
You are my heroes*

Books in the *Untwisting Scriptures* series

*Untwisting Scriptures
that were used to tie you up, gag you,
and tangle your mind*

*Book 1: Rights, Bitterness, and Taking Up Offenses
Book 2: Patriarchy and Authority
Book 3: Your Words, Your Emotions*

*Untwisting Scriptures
to Find Freedom and Joy in Jesus Christ*

Book 4: Wolves, Hypocrisy, Sin Leveling, and Righteousness

Go to heresthejoy.com to download your own copy of my free Guide, *How to Enjoy the Bible Again after Spiritual Abuse (without feeling guilty or getting triggered out of your mind).*

.

Contents

1. Why I'm Talking about Patriarchy..5
PART ONE: The Problem of "Biblical Patriarchy"
2. "Biblical Patriarchy": Here's How You Replaced God 11
3. The Clash of Kingdoms.. 17
4. *The Return of the Daughters* Meets Rachael Denhollander....23
5. To Those in "Biblical Patriarchy": Return to God 29
PART TWO "Children Obey Your Parents" (All the Time in Every Way and Forever)
6. Doug Phillips under the Old Covenant 41
7. "Children Obey Your Parents"?...57
8. "(Adult) Children Obey Your Parents"? For Adults Raised in "Biblical Patriarchy"..65
9. The King, the Prisoner, the Soldier, and Jesus 79
10. Rebellion is the Sin like Witchcraft 89
11. "You Just Need to Be Content" 95
PART THREE: The Problem of Church "Authorities"
12. The Umbrella Heresy—at Home and Church 103
13. Your Pastor is Not Moses: a Response to John Bevere's *Under Cover*... 119
14. That "Obey Your Leaders and Submit to Their Authority" Scripture: Examining Hebrews 13:17................................129
15. "Loyalty" is Not a Christian Virtue 147
PART FOUR: The Authority of Jesus . . . and Us
16. Jesus vs. the Pharisees... 155
17. Thoughts for the Hopeless from Isaiah 40 161
18. The Authority We Have in Jesus Christ 167
Appendix A: Examining the Matriarchs of Patriarchy 187
Appendix B: Further Questions and Answers on "Children Obey Your Parents"..201
Scripture Index...207

CHAPTER 1

Why I'm Talking about Patriarchy

THE MODERN MOVEMENT of so-called "Biblical" patriarchy really has nothing to do with the patriarchs of the Bible.

The word "patriarch" is found in only two places in the Bible: Acts 2:29 in reference to David and in Hebrews 7:4 in reference to Abraham. Those are two of the primary Old Testament saints we Christians can look to as examples of faithful living.

David and Abraham weren't called "patriarchs" until one or two thousand years after they lived, so by that time they had earned titles of distinction. The people of this modern movement have not.

It's important when we discuss a concept, to be sure we agree on what the concept means. For this term, "Biblical *patriarchy*," sometimes abbreviated to just "patriarchy," I'm referring to a very specific sub-movement within the larger movement of homeschooling that launched around the time *Patriarch Magazine* was first published in 1991.

And what's more, this modern patriarchy movement is an extreme form of a twisted teaching that has long been prevalent and deep rooted in conservative U.S. church culture (and perhaps that of other Western churches). Though presented as valuing women and children, the bottom-line teaching is that women are too emotional and gullible to seek God on their own. So God always works through "the patriarchs"—that is, the husband and father (and/or the pastor)—to reveal His will for those beneath them.

I still have the premier issue of *Patriarch Magazine*, which I ordered as gift for my husband, since, coming from a home that was perhaps more of a matriarchy, I was very eager to have a "Biblical home." (I also ordered another one called *Quit You Like Men* that I probably also still have.) My husband, wise for a young man in his early 30s, told me that something seemed off about this philosophy and he had no interest in it.

So that was the end of that, since I figured it would be a bit too ironic for a woman to pursue patriarchy whose husband didn't agree with it.[1] We didn't become part of the movement called "Biblical patriarchy."[2]

Through those years in my 30s and 40s I led a homeschool group, and now I know some of the patriarchy people were in it. But I wasn't fully aware of what they believed, taught, and practiced. They were conservative in dress and other standards, and so was I, and that was about all I knew.

No, that wasn't quite all. In those years I faithfully attended the annual statewide homeschool conventions. I dreamed about someday being a speaker for one of the small workshops (maybe one day, for example, I would be able to talk about how to keep

---

[1] I didn't know at that time about the Matriarchs of Patriarchy. But now they're in Appendix A.

[2] We also didn't become an Advanced Training Institute (Gothard) family, for the same reason—I was super excited to do it, but my cautious husband didn't want another man telling us how to run our home.

your home organized, because maybe one day I would actually have an organized home).

I remember hearing a very young Doug Phillips of Vision Forum speak at the conventions, thinking that something was "off" about him (it felt like arrogance), and losing interest in hearing him further. But somehow I got on the Vision Forum catalog mailing list.

I never ordered from the Vision Forum catalog. The $89.00 coonskin caps and such were obviously designed for wealthy people and seemed to me to be ridiculous ways to spend hard-earned money. I laughed, and I showed them to my family so they could laugh too.

But it all seemed harmless.

In 2005 when we had newly moved to Greenville, South Carolina, we visited many churches in order to get a feel for the spiritual condition of the area. One of them I now know was a patriarchal church, though I couldn't have articulated it at that time.

I saw a disturbing shadow over the face of one of the elders' wives, but in those days of my ignorance I couldn't understand it. Besides that, my main takeaway from that strange church was their emphatic determination to keep unsaved people out, lest their children be tainted.

A year or two later, I met a new friend who had escaped from an abusive husband (the first friend to educate me about domestic abuse in the Christian world). She visited that church, and was told by the elders there that a wife was obligated to stay with her husband even if he killed her and the children.

Though I didn't have words to connect the pieces, this was the beginning of my education in the darkness of the modern patriarchy movement.

Then when it came to having words, the internet changed everything.

In 2008 through a few new blogs, I began to be peripherally aware of cult-like behavior in Christian environments. In 2010 I was drawn into the "Christian abuse" blogs again. But I thought, well, I didn't know any of those people, and I turned my attention back to my family, where I needed to focus at that time.

In 2012 it happened again, and this time there was no turning back, because of a new deep-level and very personal awareness of sexual abuse in the Christian world. By then, a proliferation of blogs addressed abuse not only in the Bob Jones University sphere (my primary sphere at the time), but other Christian worlds, including the world of "Biblical patriarchy."

I researched. It was clear that at the very least, spiritual abuse and hypocrisy prospered in this environment. And from what I saw, it looked like it could be the cover for far darker things. As I read about the movement that had been blooming for years with flowers and stunning, rosy-cheeked girls, and lovely dresses with matching hair bows and daddy-daughter parties, my stomach turned.

As I followed the fall of Vision Forum's Doug Phillips in ignominy,[3] I learned more and more about what was behind the movement, what had been promulgated in those families and churches, and what . . . what . . . what in the world . . . was going on.

And I began to meet those who had lived through it.

---

[3] The primary source from which I learned about Doug Phillips was www.SpiritualSoundingBoard.com, founded by Julie Anne Smith. The Doug Phillips posts are here: https://spiritualsoundingboard.com/?s=doug+phillips

PART ONE

The Problem of "Biblical Patriarchy"

CHAPTER 2

"Biblical Patriarchy": Here's How You Replaced God

"EVERYTHING CAME TO a head in my mid-twenties," she was saying. "So that's when I finally got out." She balanced her young child on her knee as she spoke. "I want to help others get out."

I was having tea with a daughter of patriarchy.

She told me one story after another, about her own life and the lives of others, about control and domination and refusal to allow independent thinking, and for some, eventual escapes.

"So, of all the ones you know who got out," I asked, "how many are still following Christ?"

My new friend paused, figuring. "I guess three out of about thirty that I know for sure."

Three out of thirty. Ten percent were still following Jesus.

She was one of that ten percent. She was one of the small minority who had left this system but still looked for freedom and hope and truth in the Christ who is shown in the Scriptures and through the Spirit.

I thought about the young people the parents of "Biblical patriarchy" used to be, when we all sat in homeschool conventions together in the 1980s and 1990s, the air crackling with the energy of hope and optimism that we would raise up a godly generation.

What had happened in those intervening years? How had so many of them gone so far astray as to think oppression, manipulation, threats, and control were part of the right way to raise their children, especially their daughters, in godliness?

"My father told me so often that God works through men to reveal his will for women. My parents nailed me with it before I left home: 'You can't know God's will without a father or husband. Women are too easily deceived. They cannot trust their own hearts.'"[4]

I'm not saying that oppression, manipulation, threats, and control this extreme are present in every "Biblical patriarchal" family. But it's been the case in the majority of the ones I've heard about.

But the root problem . . . the root problem isn't that oppression. It isn't that control.

The root problem of God's Old Covenant people

God's Old Covenant people were oppressors too. Their sin of oppression is described in the Old Testament prophets—Scriptures in Isaiah and Jeremiah give several examples.[5] (And as a side note, among the beautiful promises God made in these books

---

[4] A commenter on the blog post version of this chapter responded to this statement this way: "'Women are too easily deceived.' If (IF!!) we are too easily deceived, it is because we have been indoctrinated by a cult-like group, that it's ok for the patriarchy to control us. It's idolatry. That's where the deceit is. But now we know better."

[5] For example, Isaiah 1:4 and Jeremiah 1:16; 2:12-13, 17, 19; 5:3, 7, 19; 8:5, 17:13; 19:4; 22:9.

is that those who mourned—that is, the oppressed—would be comforted.)

But what did God say was the root problem, in Jeremiah 2:13?

You have forsaken Me.

The root problem of "Biblical patriarchy"

The root problem in "Biblical patriarchy" for many of its adherents is that while lip service was being given to Jesus Christ—or maybe I should say to God, since many of them don't mention Jesus a whole lot—He Himself was removed from the place of centrality and supremacy in their individual lives, their families, and their churches.

Maybe they said, "I did all those things wrong when I was a teenager, so now I'm going to follow these rules and make my children follow these rules, so they won't do any of those wrong things. They won't make any of those mistakes."

Did they put a system in the center of their lives where the Jesus Christ belonged?

In my mulling and pondering, I remembered a significant incident from my own life in about 2002.

My own experience with this replacement

I was asked to speak at a gathering of about 200 homeschooling mothers, at an annual "ladies' luncheon and curriculum sale." The leader, whom I had recently met, asked several different local women to speak every year.

I recall that an encouraging friend said to me, "Maybe after you do this, you'll get asked to speak other places too."

When I asked the leader what I should speak on, she said, "Whatever the Lord lays on your heart."

Well, indeed there was something the Lord had been laying on my heart. It was a phenomenon I was observing in the homeschooling world that I figured was simply an error, a mistake that needed a reminder.

I worked for many days on my hour-long talk, with much prayer, making posters and cut-outs (that would look oh-so-archaic now) with this theme:

Don't forget that Jesus Christ should be at the center of your life. Don't make the mistake of letting your husband or your children take that center role. As homeschoolers it's so easy for us to fall into this error, so we need to keep recalibrating our hearts toward Him.

I dressed it up with funny stories and passionate examples and all the rest, but in my mind I knew all I was doing was reminding them of truth. *I knew I was telling them something they already knew.*

But as it turned out, I was wrong. As it turned out, I was saying something extremely controversial.

Afterwards, my encouraging friend said, "That was really good. But a whole lot of women here aren't going to like it."

I was taken aback. "Why?" I mean, this was just something obvious and extremely non-controversial. How could they possibly disagree with it?

"Because they believe their husbands should be at the center of their lives."

I remember staring at her, wondering if she was joking. "You're kidding," I said.

"No, I'm not. That's what they believe."

Now, that story shows you how clueless I was. And the word *patriarchy* was never mentioned. But that was what I was up against.

I'm sure after she heard me speak, the leader had second thoughts about inviting women to speak on whatever the Lord laid on their heart.

At the time, I didn't follow up on the mystery of it all, maybe because I felt intimidated, maybe because my life was full with homeschooling and caring for a mother-in-law with Alzheimer's.

And because I didn't, I never really investigated what my friend was referring to about wives and husbands. That is, not until years later when I began to read online about the problems with "Biblical patriarchy," from the people who were coming out of it.

And yes, it's really idolatry

Some would say the most basic problem is the idolatry of the man and the man wanting to be treated as god.

But I believe that isn't the most fundamental problem.

The first problem is *leaving the true God*.

I've blogged about idolatry and how I wish Christians wouldn't be so quick to accuse themselves and others of it. (Among other things, don't confuse idolatry with grief, fear, or doubt, don't think all Christians are idol factories, and don't think that every sin has to have an idol at its base.)

But idolatry is real when someone consciously puts something else at the center of his life, where Jesus Christ alone belongs, as the case of any woman who willfully does this with her husband.

It's idolatry even if you think that person or thing you're putting at the center is going to help you reach God.

After all, that's what all the idols of any religion are about.

Jesus Christ is the only right way to reach God. There is to be no one between you and Him.

A clash of kingdoms

"My father told me so often that God works through men to reveal his will for women. 'You can't know God's will without a father or husband.'"

What this patriarchal teaching is saying is that *a woman is only to consider the desires of her father or husband.* She is not to seek God on her own.

What danger comes with this unbiblical teaching!

Whose kingdom will be promoted? The Kingdom of God or the kingdom of man? Will Jesus Christ be both central and supreme for each one of His people?

CHAPTER 3

The Clash of Kingdoms

IN 2013 I SAW with grief that one of the Patriarchs of Patriarchy had fallen, and his organization along with it. That was Doug Phillips, head of Vision Forum (the $89.00 coonskin cap promoters).

My grief was not because I thought Doug Phillips incapable of falling—far from it—but because I grieved for the many people who put so much faith in him, and especially for the women and children who have been genuinely victimized—spiritually, emotionally, and physically—in the Patriarchy Movement.

The beautiful Botkin sisters

As this scandal led me to delve deeper into research about "Biblical patriarchy," I again came across the beautiful Botkin sisters. I had first learned of Anna Sophia and Elizabeth Botkin at a time when they epitomized the way of "Biblical patriarchy" to many single young women.

The sisters had written a book, *So Much More: The Remarkable Influence of Visionary Daughters on the Kingdom of God,*[6] when they were 17 and 19. In 2013 when I wrote my blog post about them, the Botkin sisters were ages 28 and 30 and unmarried,

---

[6] Vision Forum, 2005.

staying at home and serving their father. Now, in 2021, they are 36 and 38, staying at home and serving their father, having had more than one suitor turned away.

Their story is not uncommon in the "Biblical patriarchy" world.

What the Botkin sisters outlined in their book and still espouse[7] is for young unmarried girls like themselves—to achieve *So Much More* than the modern culture, stay at home until marriage. Until you marry, serve your father.

Besides "submitting to his whims," "reverencing and adoring him," they have spent many years serving their own father, by speaking and writing on the importance of unmarried girls staying home and serving their fathers.

In many cases, it can be good for a young unmarried woman to stay home (though this concept of "serving the father" goes to exaggerated and disturbing lengths). But it is not a Biblical mandate. The Botkin sisters—and all of "Biblical patriarchy" along with them—have been teaching that if a woman isn't building the Kingdom of the Man in her life, she will be building Her Own Kingdom. There is no other option.[8]

All that they do—if I understand them correctly—they do for the glory of their father, not for the glory of the Lord Jesus Christ.

---

[7] www.botkinsisters.com.

[8] In response to the situation with Doug Phillips that led to his fall (a sexually abusive and exploitive relationship with his children's nanny), I wrote in a comment on my blog, "Apparently at least in some circles in Patriarchy—the highest circles—it's considered desirable for an unmarried daughter to go to work for another man as long as he is a leader in Patriarchy and doesn't pay her, because the privilege of being able to be around him is payment enough. If a nanny were paid by the family she lives with, then she would just be an employee, which would completely go against everything Patriarchy teaches. If she works for nothing, then she is serving her father by working for the high exalted leader."

They may say, "But glorifying our father IS the way we glorify Christ." But is it really?

Let's consider. Some fathers begin to enjoy having the glory for themselves. Some fathers have convinced their children to submit to nightmarish horrors in the name of submitting to them as representatives of God.

The two must be separated, especially as young women reach adulthood and develop their own relationship with their Savior, apart from their father (or mother) as intermediary.

Women who have done exploits

I tossed and turned one night, thinking about all this. When I had first begun pondering patriarchy and the work of the Botkin sisters, I was writing two series of missionary books. One told the story of Margaret Nicholl, one of the first missionaries to the Central African Republic.[9] A young unmarried woman, Margaret saw God do great things there (and incidentally, met her husband there).

Several of my missionary books have referenced the work of another woman, Joy Ridderhof, who in fact never married, but instead founded the ministry called Gospel Recordings, which has been of incalculable value to missionaries from the 1940s even to the present day.[10]

According to the beautiful Botkins and the Patriarchy Movement as a whole, both of these missionary women, along with many others such as the intrepid Amy Carmichael (whom I also

---

[9] Rebecca Davis, *The Good News Must Go Out: True Stories of God at Work in the Central African Republic,* Hidden Heroes #2, Christian Focus Publications, 2011.

[10] Rebecca Davis, *Joy Ridderhof: Voice Catcher around the World,* Potter's Wheel #3, Pennycress Publications, 2015.

wrote a book about!), were outside the will of God. All of them should have stayed home under their fathers.

"Missions" according to Patriarchy

Yes, the "Biblical patriarchists" do give a nod to missions. They teach in their two-hundred-year plan that Christianity will dominate the world. But this plan appears to be eerily similar to the way Muslims teach that Islam will dominate the world: by having a lot of children.[11] Building their earthly dynasties, they called themselves Quiverfull families, based on Psalm 127:3-5.

> *Behold, children are a heritage from the LORD,*
> *The fruit of the womb is a reward.*
> *Like arrows in the hand of a warrior,*
> *So are the children of one's youth.*
> *Happy is the man who has his quiver full of them;*
> *They shall not be ashamed,*
> *But shall speak with their enemies in the gate.*

The work of the flesh vs. the work of the Spirit

On her quiet little blog that dropped like a bombshell on the "Biblical patriarchy" world in 2009, Hillary McFarland wrote,

> *Many proponents see this [Scripture] as a call to bear an army for the Lord by raising a multitude of those who will call upon His name. In the war against culture—so prevalent within Evangelical and Fundamentalist circles—the understanding is that through sheer numbers of godly offspring, our culture*

---

[11] Back in the 1990s when I didn't know I was listening to patriarchal thinking, I remember hearing a fellow homeschooler saying that wanting to have more children was a "godly desire." Actually, this might or might not be a godly desire. It might be a desire born of peer pressure or pride.

> can be redeemed in the name of Christ. In the interest of balance, I would like to issue a humble reminder.

[Here she quoted Ephesians 6:10-18.]

> *These Scriptures remind us that the war on culture, this spiritual battle against the principalities, powers, and the rulers of the darkness of this age, cannot be waged through the efforts of the flesh. It is essential to remain vigilant, for the enemy who prowls like a lion comes many times cloaked in righteous attire. When we lose focus upon the crux of our mission, replacing the commandments of Jesus Himself with that which has the appearance of holiness, the enemy has secured a victory, as temporary as it may be.* [12]

As I observed on my own blog in 2013, the Kingdom of Islam has got us beat hands down when it comes to taking over the world by having children. By birth, Muslims are winning, and until Christians advocate polygamy, we won't be able to catch up.[13]

But do you know what religion is winning the growth race when it comes to *conversions*?

Christianity.

There is no contest here—Christianity is the clear winner. Through the opening of the eyes of the blind—yes, even Muslims—Jesus Christ is being glorified, and His Kingdom is spreading throughout the earth. This is what I've written books about.

However, for a young unmarried woman in "Biblical patriarchy," life is not about building the Kingdom of Jesus Christ through the powerful spread of His glorious Gospel of Grace.

---

[12] https://quiveringdaughters.blogspot.com/2009/03/quiverfull-of-thoughts.html

[13] The predictions of this short video (from 2007) are fascinating. https://www.youtube.com/watch?v=6-3X5hIFXYU

It can't be, because then there might be a conflict between Christ and her Earthly Father. The Kingdom of her Earthly Father must be supreme.

The war God is fighting is not the culture war that patriarchy teaches. It is not about "the world" that must never darken the doors of "the chosen." It is not about "feminism" vs. "true womanhood."

This is a battle of kingdoms.

Instead of focusing on the Kingdom of Man, we must focus on the Kingdom of the mighty Savior Jesus Christ, through His glorious Gospel of Grace.

He is the transformer of lives.

His is the Kingdom that matters.

CHAPTER 4

The Return of the Daughters Meets Rachael Denhollander

IN 2012 I WAS newly aware of the sexual abuse that was and is rampant in our churches. As I read about the often bizarre and truly unhealthful relationships being promoted between fathers and daughters in the "Biblical patriarchy" movement, I thought, "Someday I may find out about father-daughter incest in some of these families." It seemed obvious.

And I couldn't have been more right. I didn't see then the darker things I would learn about (sex trafficking, sexual abuse by mothers, etc.), but at least I could see that much.

Sexual abuse in *The Return of the Daughters*

But back in 2008 . . . the video documentary that the Botkin sisters had produced, *The Return of the Daughters* didn't ignore sexual abuse. No, in fact, the story was referenced of Jacob's daughter Dinah (Genesis 34), who was sexually assaulted by a city leader.

Then this story was used to prove their point—if she had stayed at home with her father, this wouldn't have happened to her.

And this is where Rachael Denhollander comes in.

Rachael Denhollander's reaction

Rachael is the Christian who worked relentlessly through 2016 and 2017 to expose the abuse of an Olympic doctor, Larry Nassar, providing the encouragement for over 200 other Nassar victims and survivors to speak out.

In 2008 Rachael had already been sexually assaulted by this doctor multiple times as a teen and was now a woman in her twenties, teaching, going to law school . . . and attending a family camp with her soon-to-be fiancé Jacob.

I'm quoting from her book, *What is a Girl Worth?* (which I highly recommend) about what was taught at that camp.

> *At some point, one of the presenters decided that showing a video documentary titled <u>The Return of the Daughters</u> would be an excellent complement to that year's message, the camp's purpose, and the beliefs of these families. . . . [O]ne of the men teaching in the film turned his attention to the rape of Dinah—a story from the Old Testament about a woman who [was] raped while visiting women in town. Her brothers avenge[d] her, while her father [did] nothing.*
>
> *As soon as I heard the name Dinah come out of the teacher's mouth, I went stiff. I knew exactly where this was heading. I'd heard it so many times before. Don't go there. No no no no no.*
>
> *But he did. This rape, this abuse, he taught, is what happens when a daughter steps outside her father's protection.*
>
> *I wanted to scream. It was a lie from the pit of hell, and I knew*

4 – RETURN OF DAUGHTERS RACHAEL DENHOLLANDER

> *the damage it would do. No one else moved or registered any concern. I'd been here before. Abuse is the woman's fault. It's a common assumption that if you are abused, it's because you did something wrong.*
>
> *No blame on the rapist. No guilt for the father who shrugged it off. It's the daughter's fault. This is what happens to girls who . . . .*
>
> *Damaged. And it's your fault.*[14]

Notice she'd "heard it so many times before." From other leaders who taught this very thing about this very story.[15]

I wrote to Anna Sofia and Elizabeth Botkin to ask them if they would like to make a statement about their documentary *The Return of the Daughters*. This would seem wise, considering Rachael's critique and considering that several young women whose stories were told in that documentary now have lives that look significantly different from what was portrayed there.

I hoped they would consider saying something publicly about the error of a teaching that implies that simply staying in her father's home under the care of her father will keep a girl safe in every way, even from sexual assault.[16]

---

[14] Rachael Denhollander, *What is a Girl Worth? My Story of Breaking the Silence and Exposing the Truth about Larry Nassar and USA Gymnastics*. Tyndale, 2019, pp. 125-126.

[15] For example, *Institute in Basic Youth Conflicts, Character Sketches from the Pages of Scripture, Illustrated in the World of Nature, Volume 1*. The Institute, 1976, pp 287-289.

[16] They did reply, asking me to take the quotation in context. I did, and Doug Phillips' commentary on Numbers chapter 30, and my commentary on his commentary, now have become Chapter 6.

It didn't protect Rachael Denhollander, even though she has loving parents who have supported her every step of the way in her fight against these crimes.

Praying for a return of the daughters

And for those who don't have loving supportive parents? For those whose parents have even sexually assaulted them? I wondered if the Botkin women knew: so many have been so deeply harmed in outwardly "Christian" homes that this is one of the primary reasons young adults walk away from Christianity.

In fact, sometimes the worst danger of all is in the father's home. We ignore it to our peril.

One of my deepest prayers is for those precious souls who have been harmed by the evil ones using Christianity as a façade—those precious souls who are now moving in any direction but Jesus. I pray that these wounded ones will see and know the truth, that no matter what destructive teachings they have been taught, they'll see that Jesus Christ is indeed their only hope.

He is our only hope.

Our Lord Jesus can save them from their sin, He can rescue them from the shame they carry and are trying desperately to escape, and He can heal and cleanse them thoroughly.

And as satisfying as it was for over 200 women to see the Olympic-athlete doctor child molester Larry Nassar brought down,[17] there is more.

We as the people of God fighting for these souls in the Name of Jesus . . .

. . . we will one day see all the evil ones brought down at His feet.

---

[17] The story of his downfall is detailed in *What Is a Girl Worth?*

4 – RETURN OF DAUGHTERS RACHAEL DENHOLLANDER

I pray that many daughters of "Biblical patriarchy" who have wandered because of horrors done to them in the Name of Jesus will return to the loving Shepherd of their souls.

That is the Return of the Daughters for which I pray.

CHAPTER 5

To Those in "Biblical Patriarchy": Return to God

WHAT DOES THE Kingdom of God look like? Regarding the vertical relationship, Jesus said,

> *Love the Lord your God with all your heart, soul, mind, and strength.* (Matthew 22:37)

And regarding the horizontal relationships He said,

> *You know the rulers of the Gentiles lord it over them, and their great men exercise authority over them. But it is not this way among you. But whoever wishes to become great among you shall be your servant.* (Matthew 20:25-26)

Love and service, not earthly "lordship": this is what the Kingdom of God looks like.

Who is worthy to receive power and wealth and wisdom and strength and honor and glory and praise? Revelation 5:12 says it is the Lord of that transcendent Kingdom, Jesus Christ.

And in relation to that Kingdom, "We ought to obey God rather than men," said the apostles in Acts 5:29.

When there is a disparity between the will of God and the will of man, then the will of God holds sway.

These are kingdoms in conflict.

Broken cisterns for living water

So many of my generation, the generation that caused the air to crackle with the energy of hope and enthusiasm at those early homeschool conventions, put something else at the center of their lives and their ministries. They made something else the focus of their hopes. So many of them expected to find LIFE in something other than Jesus Christ alone.

> *Be appalled, O heavens, at this;*
>   *be shocked, be utterly desolate,*
> *declares the Lord,*
> *for my people have committed two evils:*
> *they have forsaken me, the fountain of living waters,*
> *and hewed out cisterns for themselves,*
>   *broken cisterns that can hold no water.*
> (Jeremiah 2:12-13)

I'm appalled, with the heavens, horrified and dumbfounded. I never imagined, those years ago, that this would happen.

What are their broken cisterns?

A system

They put their trust in the system of "Biblical patriarchy," thinking if they would cleave to the system, all would turn out well.

"If we just work harder at keeping the rules and commands, all will be well. All will surely be well. God will see the works of our own hands and surely bless them."

5 – TO THOSE IN "BIBLICAL PATRIARCHY": RETURN TO GOD

It is very tempting to look for a "formula" that will ensure that our children do not stray from God's way. Especially when "experts" trot out their lovely families (and they ARE lovely no doubt) purporting that they have found "the" way to raise children who will never stray.

This is a very attractive idea, especially when in the midst of disappointment with a child who has fallen into sin of some nature. Far too often we look to a leader who seems to have all the answers, rather than falling on our knees before the Lord, searching the scriptures for ourselves, and waiting upon the Father who loves our children even more greatly than we do.[18]

A person

They exalted the man, the flawed (and sometimes duplicitously wicked) man, the husband/father or sometimes the pastor or another leader, to the place where Jesus Himself should be. They looked to the man to give them the words of Jesus Christ, to stand in His place.

"God will surely see how much we honor the man He put in a place of authority over us, and all will surely be well. He will surely bless us."

An institution

The family became an idol, the picture-perfect family, and I mean that literally. Do you know how many patriarchal families have looked picture-perfect while all hell is breaking loose behind closed doors?

---

[18] Hillary McFarland, "Why Patriarchy Can Look Attractive," https://quiveringdaughters.blogspot.com/2010/06/why-patriarchy-can-look-attractive.html, June 2009.

"Just look at those pictures; God will surely honor how godly our family looks and all will be well and we'll raise up a godly generation if it kills us and them."

Whose kingdom will be promoted? The Kingdom of God or the kingdom of man?

Will Jesus Christ be both central and supreme for each one of His people? [19]

Return

What did God say was the root problem of the Old Covenant people who were oppressing those under them?

You have left Me.[20]

What did God say was the solution?

Return to Me.[21]

Back in chapter 2 I mentioned having tea with a daughter of patriarchy, and I asked her how many people who had left the movement were still following Jesus.

I said *still*, even though it sounded like many of these families may never have really followed Him. After all, if a group teaches

---

[19] A commenter on my blog said: "A number of years ago our church motto was 'committed to Godly families,' which kind of bothered me for the reasons you stated. Thankfully our Pastor changed it to 'committed to Christ.' I think he saw that as important Godly families are, they are not what we should worship and make the center of our lives. He said if we make Christ the center then we will be committed to Godly families and love them as we should." Comment on www.heresthejoy.com "'Biblical' patriarchy: Here's how you replaced God." July 5, 2017.

[20] He said this in many places, such as Isaiah 1:4 and Jeremiah 1:16; 2:12-13, 17, 19; 5:3, 7, 19; 8:5, 17:13; 19:4; 22:9.

[21] He said this in many places, such as Isaiah 55:7 and Jeremiah 3:22; 4:1; 18:11; 35:15; 36:3; and 36:7.

"the only way to know God's will for your life is through a husband or father" then I believe they're teaching heresy.

And heresy so central to the truth of what Christianity actually is that they could be considered a cult.

After all, 1 Timothy 2:5 says,

> *For there is one God, and there is one mediator between God and men, the man Christ Jesus*

My new friend, the daughter of patriarchy, had told me that of all her peers, only ten percent were following Jesus. Another friend confirmed that statistic.

So after we parted and I got to a quiet place, I wept.

I wept for the young people, those in the ninety percent, who think what they've left is Christianity, when in many cases it isn't Christianity at all, but only a twisted, misshapen copy, a hollow echo of it.

I wept for the many parents who as young people themselves had joyfully embraced "Biblical patriarchy" as God's truth. If in those days they could have foreseen what they would become, what they would fall prey to, many of them would have turned away in horror.

The horror of it

> *Be appalled, O heavens, at this;*
> *be shocked, be utterly desolate,*
> *declares the Lord,*
> *for my people have committed two evils:*
> *they have forsaken me, the fountain of living waters,*
> *and hewed out cisterns for themselves,*
> *broken cisterns that can hold no water.*
> *(Jeremiah 2:12-13)*

A call to the parents ... to return

Return, return, I call to my generation who are stuck in the idolatry of a system, a person, and an institution. I cry out to you to return to Jesus, the fountain of living waters. Shed the pharisaical baggage of the system, the person, and the institution. Look to Jesus Christ Himself and Him alone to quench your thirst, to give you hope, to provide your salvation.

Repent. That is, come to your senses to see that the way you were going was wrong, and to turn to go the right way.

Take your hands off your adult children's shoulders and look to the Holy Spirit (Yes! Remember Him?) to do a life-giving work in the hearts of your children—and in your own.

A call to the ninety percent ... to come

To those who have departed Christianity because you equated it with the terrible oppression you experienced, which many Christians haven't taken seriously . . . some of us are taking it very seriously.

It may be that you departed from an idolatry where Christ was never mentioned except as one more rule-giver, as one more example you could never live up to, as one more teacher of "submission," as one more way to beat you over the head. . . .

I want to tell you, that is not Christianity. As I cry out to your parents to return, I cry out to you to come.

Come to the one you never knew, who really does offer beauty for ashes and the oil of joy for mourning, who really does offer deliverance for captives and the binding up of the brokenhearted.

Come see who Jesus really is.

A call to young adults under the system ... to listen to His voice

There's one more group I want to speak to. It is to adults who are still living under the authority of patriarchal parents. You feel stuck, but you want to honor your parents.

I plead with you, don't be guilty of the idolatry of parents. Don't, in the name of honoring, displace the Lord Jesus Christ, your rightful Sovereign, in your life.

It can be confusing, I know, trying to sort it out. It can be confusing, when maybe you're told that if you don't obey everything your parents say, then you're guilty of rebellion (and of course we know "rebellion is as the sin of witchcraft").[22] It can even seem terrifying.

But seek Jesus in the deepest places of your heart. Seek Him through His holy Word, get to know who He really is. Ask for His Holy Spirit to open your eyes as you read the Scriptures. The Holy Spirit—He may not be mentioned much in your family, but if you have trusted in Christ, He is the power of the living Christ in you.

The hope of glory is not having a picture-perfect family.

The hope of glory is Christ in you.

Be willing to honor your parents in the ultimate way, by honoring and following God. Love Jesus and be willing to suffer being misunderstood, maligned, and persecuted for His Name.

On Hillary McFarland's Quivering Daughter's blog, guest author Jim Karpowitz wrote,

> *May I suggest, dear sister [or brother], that if your heart is tender toward Him and you left an unhealthy situation, then you haven't left Him. Guilt, shame, manipulation,*

---

[22] This Scripture is addressed in chapter 10.

> domination, authoritarian control and abuse are not legitimate, biblical ways for a family to operate. Those dynamics might try to follow you out the door but being free of them will be the path to a relationship with God that you never thought you could have. . . . Reach out to Jesus with your pain and know that He reaches out to you in grace and mercy, even if you didn't see that modeled in a supposedly Christian environment.[23]

For me to see that I'm writing those words about my own generation, those people who stood around me at the homeschool conventions, some of whom may have bought some of the books I've written, is nearly mind-boggling to me. But if a system goes as far astray as this one seems to have gone, the system will need to be forsaken in order to truly follow Jesus Christ. This won't be the first time it's happened in history.

When it's time, it's possible to leave well (and I pray you can connect with Spirit-filled Christ-lovers on the outside who will help you do so), still honoring your parents in the ways that truly matter, without uttering words you'll later regret, leaving to truly follow Jesus rather than simply to follow your own way.

I pray with you that lost relationships will one day be restored, based on the love and joy of Jesus Christ rather than on earthly authorities and earthly systems and earthly idols.

I pray to our Father God that His Son Jesus Christ, King of heaven and earth, will truly reign in the hearts of those who have worshipped a system, a person, or an institution instead of the Savior of the world. I pray that He and He alone will be glorified in the lives of those who claim His Name.

O Lord God, speed that day.

---

[23] Jim Karpowitz, "Considering a Godly Response to Unhealthy Authority," https://quiveringdaughters.blogspot.com/2009/12/considering-godly-response-to-unhealthy.html, December 2009.

5 – TO THOSE IN "BIBLICAL PATRIARCHY": RETURN TO GOD

There's a spring of living water,
As fresh as love, as clear as truth, and never bitter.
And some have tasted of that water
And decided they'd rather hew themselves a cistern.

And the cistern—it is broken,
And the people they are choking
In the mud at the bottom of their hole.

Return, oh return to the water!
Return and let your soul be satisfied.
Return, oh return to your lover!
Then in Him will be your glory forever.

And the spring is still beside them
More alive than life itself and strong as thunder.
But they won't turn,
Though their tongues are dry and swollen.
Even the heavens, they look down on them and wonder.

They're afraid and horrified
That the people have despised
The light that was sparkling before them.

Return, oh return to the water!
Return and let your soul be satisfied.
Return oh return to your lover!
Then in Him will be your glory forever.
Then in Him will be your glory forever.[24]

---

[24] "Return to the Waters," words and music copyright © by Christiana Mayfield Music, 2013. Used by permission.

PART TWO

"Children Obey Your Parents" (All the Time in Every Way and Forever)

CHAPTER 6

Doug Phillips under the Old Covenant

WHEN I CHALLENGED the Botkin sisters about the views their documentary taught about Jacob's daughter Dinah, they asked me to take the Dinah quotation in context. So I'm including the entire quotation here, from Vision Forum founder Doug Phillips.

> *One of the most interesting chapters in the Bible is Numbers chapter 30, which is a rich depository of instruction for fathers and daughters. Here in Numbers chapter 30 we see an interesting legal question arise.*
>
> *What happens if a daughter goes out and makes a contract, or she makes an oath or a vow, but she wasn't approved of her father? What happens? Here's what the Bible says. If the father discovers that either his wife or his daughter who still lives under his roof and under his protection and care have gone out and have covenanted or contracted or vowed without his consent in a manner that is inconsistent with the direction of the household, he has the ability to nullify that. On the other hand, if he doesn't nullify it in the day in which he hears it, he ratifies it and approves it.*
>
> *Now what does this mean? Why is this important? Well it's important because what it tells you is that the family is a unified whole. That the father is the head of the home. And that both the wife and the daughter are not independent*

individuals, but that they are agents of the father. Now we see this in Proverbs 31, where the woman is going out and the husband has no need of spoil; in fact, he is in the gates of the land, he is a leader, because he trusts his wife, who manages the affairs well, and he is even engaged in amazing acts of entrepreneurship.

But if the father did not authorize that, then those contracts and those vows would not stand. Well, the implications of this include some of the following ideas.

Number 1. Daughters aren't to be independent. They are not to act outside the scope of their father as long as they're under the authority of their fathers, fathers have the ability to nullify—or not—the oaths and the vows. Daughter can't just go out and independently say, "I'm going to marry whoever I want." No, the father has the ability to say, "No, I'm sorry, that has to be approved by me." She can't even go out and represent him on a business level unless the father says, "Yes, you're authorized and you're approved by me."

Is this some sort of oppressive patriarchalism? Absolutely not. This is order. This is love. This is integrity. Because what it means is instead of a whole bunch of individuals living under one house, you have a unified structure, you have a unified whole with a God-appointed head. It also means protection for everyone else out there. It means order for society itself, and it's a great blessing.

And so what we see from Numbers 30 is the presumption, "My daughter's at home, under the roof of my house, protected by the father."

What we see from Numbers chapter 30 is that there are even legal oath-based covenant-based implications for this. Daughters need the approval of their dads to marry. Unless of course the fathers say, "Daughter, get out of here, I release you from my authority." The problem is we don't see any example of that in the entire Bible. We don't see a principle that leads us to that conclusion. We see no precepts. We see no patterns.

And the only examples we see are negative examples where fathers let their daughters out and they find themselves in peril. Dinah would be one example, a daughter that went out unprotected and was raped, and brought devastation on the family line. That's not to suggest that would always happen, only that the Bible is replete with examples of daughters under the roof of their protecting fathers, and it's completely absent of any examples or principles that lead us to think that it's normative for a daughter just to go out on her own. Numbers 30 says, "Daughters, you're under the authority of your dads."[25]

Our hope and faith as we read the Scriptures

Before I reply to Doug Phillips' teaching, let me say something I hope will be as freeing to you as it has been to me.

After Jesus' resurrection and before his ascension, He appeared to his disciples. "Then he opened their minds to understand the Scriptures." (Luke 24:45)

The disciples had been taught the Old Testament Scriptures their entire lives. They had followed Jesus Himself for three years. But only when He opened their minds did they begin to understand. Only when the risen Christ gave them eyes to see did they begin to recognize the shadow of the New Covenant in the Old, and to view the Old Covenant in the light of the New.

And there's more. Just before his crucifixion, Jesus told his disciples about "the Helper, the Holy Spirit, whom the Father will send in my name." Jesus also called this Helper "the Spirit of

---

[25] Doug Phillips, *The Return of the Daughters: A vision of victory for the single woman of the 21st century.* Documentary film directed by Anna Sophia and Elizabeth Botkin. Western Conservatory of the Arts & Sciences, 2007.

truth," saying to them and to us, he "will be in you," "he will teach you all things," and, "he will guide you into all the truth." (John 14:17, 26; 16:13)

As you *ask* the Holy Spirit, the Helper, to enlighten your mind and heart (Ephesians 1:17-21), as you *listen* with an open heart to what the Spirit wants to teach you through His Word, we will *learn* from Christ in us, who wants to open our minds and hearts to understand the truths of the Scriptures.

Asking and listening are key. You don't have to labor to figure out what teachings seek to rightly divide the Word, and what teachings twist it. As the Holy Spirit enlightens you, these truths will become clear.[26]

As I share my response to Doug Phillips' teachings on this Scripture, I want to ask you to invite the Holy Spirit of Christ to help you discern truth from falsehood.

The lesser problem: misrepresenting life in the Old Covenant

The family is a unified whole

"The family [is ideally] a unified whole."

You see, here is truth. That's what the family is designed to be. The promise of a "unified, whole" family was one of the major appeals that led many people into patriarchy in the first place. What a shame that for most of them it didn't happen, because rules were never designed to foster an environment of love.

---

[26] This doesn't mean all Holy-Spirit-led Christians will agree on all points of doctrine. It means they'll increasingly be able to recognize which teachings exalt man and which teachings exalt God.

"Stay under your father's roof for protection"

We'll set aside for a moment the fact that this passage isn't about protection.

> *"The Bible is replete with examples of daughters under the roof of their protecting fathers."*

Certainly there are some. I'm not sure about the "roof" part in every case, but here are the ones I found:

- Rebekah, who lived with her father until Abraham's servant came to get her for Isaac (Genesis 24).
- Heman's daughters, who played timbrels (1 Chronicles 25:5-6).
- Shallum's daughters, who helped him build the city walls (Nehemiah 3:12).
- Jairus's daughter, who was raised from the dead (Matthew 9:18-25).
- Phillip's daughters, who prophesied (Acts 21:8-9).

Three out of five of those daughters (or sets of daughters) were active in their non-father-serving work, to praise God, to build the city, and to prophesy. None of those activities were "representing [her father]." Those were focused on worship of God and service for others.

Incidentally, I found just as many daughters who stayed under the "roof" of fathers who failed to receive the "protection" Phillips says they were promised:

- Jephthah's daughter, whom he offered as a sacrifice after battle (Judges 11:30-39).
- Daughters of Reuel, who were regularly attacked by nasty shepherds, without protection (Exodus 2:15-22).
- Lot's daughters, who got their father drunk and had incestuous relations with him (Genesis 19).
- Rachel, whom her father used to trick Jacob into marrying Leah (Genesis 29).

- Leah, whom her father used to trick Jacob into working for him another 7 years (Genesis 29).
- Michal, whom her father used as a pawn to try to ensnare David and get him killed (1 Samuel 18).
- Tamar, who was raped inside her father's house (Genesis 38).
- Salome, whose stepfather's lust for her drove him to fulfill her request to kill John the Baptist (Matthew 14:3-12).

Scripture shows that there is no promise or "principle" of protection if a young woman stays under her father's roof.

Extrapolation from "making vows" to "going out"

Did you notice that in Numbers chapter 30 the only thing the father was told to regulate was making vows or covenants?

So how did Doug Phillips come up with this?

> *"And the only examples we see are negative examples where fathers let their daughters out and they find themselves in peril."* (Emphasis mine.)

The fathers let their daughters out.

And yes, I'm familiar with daughters whose fathers haven't allowed them to leave the property. (Or allowed them to go out for groceries but checked the odometer before and after to make sure they went nowhere else.)

I believe this entire Scripture doesn't apply to Christians, which I'm about to explain. But *even under the Old Covenant,* fathers keeping their daughters on their own property all the time *wasn't what this was about.*

It was about making vows, contracts, and covenants.

Dinah went out to see if she could meet some friends.[27] This wasn't intrinsically a bad thing. She was innocent in it. And to be clear, the story of Dinah has nothing to do with Numbers 30.

But because Doug Phillips (and others) included it and applied it in this exposition of the Old Covenant Law, many young women became afraid to leave their parents' property without very strict rules in place.[28]

> *"[The Bible] is completely absent of any examples or principles that lead us to think that it's normative for a daughter just to go out on her own."* (Emphasis mine.)

I see this happen regularly among abusive "authorities," this bait and switch. The Bible says one thing, but then the adored, mesmerizing speaker smoothly moves it into something else.

Not allowing her to make a vow/contract/covenant on her own becomes *not allowing her to go out* on her own.

Which isn't even taught in the Old Covenant.

The greater problem: Christians are not under the Old Covenant

This is what Doug Phillips and all of the Patriarchy Movement missed. If Christians miss the many Scriptural cues that the New Covenant is better than the Old, we may read the Bible "flat," as if the Old Covenant and the New Covenant are equal and equally apply to all of us.

---

[27] Her full story is told in Genesis 34, before this law, or any Mosaic Law, was given.

[28] Or if they did, they figured they were so rebellious they might as well get their cauldrons boiling and become witches, which some of them literally have done. More in chapter 10.

If this is what you believe, I pray that you'll at least allow me a hearing in this section.[29]

Besides showing his willful ignorance of the fact that daughters are assaulted in the very homes of their fathers, sometimes by those very fathers, or in the homes of trusted leaders, even leaders of patriarchy, Doug Phillips showed his ignorance of the difference between the Old Covenant and the New Covenant.

Jesus talked about it very clearly.

> *And [Jesus] took bread, and when he had given thanks, he broke it and gave it to them, saying, "This is my body, which is given for you. Do this in remembrance of me." And likewise the cup after they had eaten, saying, "This cup that is poured out for you is the new covenant in my blood."* (Luke 22:19-20)

I write on my blog[30] about what life is like under the New Covenant of Jesus Christ, explained in the New Testament. Christians of today are the New Covenant people of God. And this is wonderful news, because the New Covenant is a different and better covenant than the Old.

> *But ... Christ has obtained a ministry that is as much more excellent than the old as the covenant he mediates is better, since it is enacted on better promises.* (Hebrews 8:6)

---

[29] I grew up under Dispensationalism, and I was active in a Reformed church for some time. I understand both perspectives well. The perspective I'm presenting here is the one I believe is most faithful to the entire Word of God.

[30] www.heresthejoy.com

Differences between the Old Covenant and the New

Here are just a few differences between the Old (Mosaic) Covenant and the New Covenant in Jesus Christ. As you read and ponder the New Testament, you'll most likely find more.

Old (Mosaic) Covenant	New Covenant in Christ	Scriptures
A physical people group. Mostly joined by physical birth.	A spiritual people group. Always joined by spiritual birth.	Ex. 19:3-6; Eph. 2:12-13; Gal. 3:29, Heb. 9:15
Covenant begun with the giving and receiving of the Mosaic Law.	Covenant begun with the giving and receiving of the wine that represented the blood of Jesus Christ, at the Last Supper.	Ex. 24:1-8, 34:27-28; Matt. 26:27-28
Covenant sealed by a physical action: circumcision.	Covenant sealed by a spiritual action: circumcision of the heart.	Ex. 12:48-49; John 7:22, Rom. 2:25-29; Col. 2:11-12
Saving faith not a prerequisite (only physical birth).	Saving faith in Jesus Christ is the only way of entrance.	Ex. 19:6; 1 Pet. 2:4-10
Exclusive to one physical people group (and those who wanted to physically join them).	Inclusive of all people groups, anyone who comes to Jesus Christ in faith.	Ex. 19:3-6; 2 Cor. 3:12-16; Eph. 2:11-22
A physical temple for physical sacrifices.	A spiritual temple (our hearts) for spiritual sacrifices (our lives consecrated to the Lord).	Heb. 9:1-5; 1 Cor. 3:16-17; 1 Pet. 2:5
A priesthood through a physical line that was constantly changing	A spiritual priesthood with a Great High Priest	Ex. 28:1-3; Heb. 2:17, 4:14-16; 1 Pet. 2:9

because of physical death.	that lives eternally and never changes.	
Full of foreshadowing and symbolism.	All symbols and shadows fulfilled and replaced with substance.	Jer. 31: 31-34, Col. 2:16-17, Heb. 10:1-2
Mosaic Law, which reveals the inability of the heart to accomplish God's law.	All of God's law fulfilled in the sinless life and atoning death of the Founder of the Covenant.	Rom. 3:20, 7:7; Heb. 7:26-28, 10:1
No mention of the Holy Spirit, except in rare exceptional cases.	Holy Spirit present and active and living in every Covenant Member.	Rom. 8:14-16, 1 Cor. 2:9-12

The importance of the Old Covenant

The Old Covenant people of God did fulfill certain important commissions.

~ Preserving the records of the holy words of God.
~ Preserving the sacrificial system that foreshadowed the final Sacrifice.
~ Preserving the prophecies leading to the coming of Jesus.
~ Preserving the genealogies for the coming of the Messiah.
~ Preserving the Law until it was fulfilled.
~ Displaying the nature of God in His holiness: showing how seriously God views sin and obedience.
~ Providing context for the coming of Jesus Christ.
~ Providing context for the outpouring of mercy and grace in the New Covenant.

The superiority of the New Covenant

~ We no longer offer sacrifices because the final Sacrifice has been offered (Hebrews 10:11-14).

- The prophecies of the first coming of Jesus have been fulfilled (Hebrews 10:5-7, 12).
- Genealogies no longer matter (Titus 3:9).
- The Law, which was never possible for anyone to keep flawlessly, has been fulfilled in Jesus Christ (Romans 10:4).
- We are no longer bound by the Old Covenant Law, but by the Law of Jesus Christ (Romans 6:14, 7:6, 13:10: Galatians 5:14).
- Jesus is better than Moses (Hebrews 3:1-6, 8:5-7).
- Jesus is better than the Old Covenant priesthood (Hebrews 8:6).

The past and the present

Doug Phillips spoke as if the situation described in Numbers 30 was current, in the present tense, but the passage he cited described laws for a situation in *history*. It should have been explained in *past tense*.[31] Like so:

> *What happened if a daughter went out and made a contract, or she made an oath or a vow, but she wasn't approved of her father? What happened? Here's what the Bible says. If the father discovered that either his wife or his daughter who still lived under his roof and under his protection and care had gone out and had covenanted or contracted or*

---

[31] I've often heard people refer to the history of the Bible in the present tense. I believe this is because they think it should be treated like literature, the way a work of fiction is handled, or a teaching that is presently available. For example, we would correctly say, "In this scene Mr. Darcy shocks Elizabeth with his expression of undying affection." We would rightly say, "In this booklet Bill Gothard tells you to get an umbrella." But if we're reading history, we would rightly say, "This video shows how Napoleon met his match at Waterloo." One day I was brought to confusion by a Chinese atheist friend who knew all the finer details of English grammar, when she challenged me that Christians refer to the "history" of the Bible in the present tense. To her this was proof that they really think of it as fiction. My only defense was that many native English speakers don't know grammar as well as she did.

> *vowed without his consent in a manner that was inconsistent with the direction of the household, he had the ability to nullify that. On the other hand, if he didn't nullify it in the day in which he heard it, he ratified it and approved it.*

In this video, Phillips describes what life was like under the Old Covenant Law. But then he extrapolates to the New Covenant believer, as if there is no difference.

There is a world of difference.

But one might say, "If it was good enough for God's people 4000 years ago, then it's good enough for me today."

God's people 4000 years ago lived in such a completely different culture that it might as well have been a different planet. Furthermore, almost all of them were so far from being the mature believers that He calls us to be that they had to be treated like little children. I've sometimes wondered (tongue in cheek) if that's why they were so often called "the children of Israel."

Paul referred to this when he wrote to the Ephesians about "growing up."

> *And he gave the apostles, the prophets, the evangelists, the shepherds and teachers, to equip the saints for the work of ministry, for building up the body of Christ, until we all attain to the unity of the faith and of the knowledge of the Son of God, to mature manhood, to the measure of the stature of the fullness of Christ,*
>
> *so that we may no longer be children, tossed to and fro by the waves and carried about by every wind of doctrine, by human cunning, by craftiness in deceitful schemes.*
>
> *Rather, speaking the truth in love, we are to grow up in every way into him who is the head, into Christ, from whom the whole body, joined and held together by every joint with which it is equipped, when each part is working properly,*

makes the body grow so that it builds itself up in love. (Ephesians 4:11-16)

Problems this confusion causes for Christians

When a New Covenant believer in Jesus Christ tries to go back to live under the Old Covenant, all manner of confusion can result, and we've seen it in the families of patriarchy.

In addition, Galatians teaches that if a Christian—truly redeemed by Jesus Christ—seeks to go back to live under the Old Covenant (under the Law, as many patriarchalists have tried to do), he will find that he is more susceptible than ever to the sins of the flesh. But as we welcome the Helper and learn from him, He helps us, not only to understand, but also to walk in His ways. Galatians 5:16-18 gives an example (emphasis mine):

> *But I say, walk by the Spirit, and you will not gratify the desires of the flesh. For the desires of the flesh are against the Spirit, and the desires of the Spirit are against the flesh, for these are opposed to each other, to keep you from doing the things you want to do. But if you are led by the Spirit, you are not under the law.*

When I began to understand this truth through a study of Galatians in 1999, I found it to be astonishing and ultimately life-changing. I later learned that it isn't only Galatians, but all of the New Testament that bears out this truth. For example, Romans 8:2-5.

> *For the law of the Spirit of life has set you free in Christ Jesus from the law of sin and death. For God has done what the law, weakened by the flesh, could not do. By sending his own Son in the likeness of sinful flesh and for sin, he condemned sin in the flesh, in order that the righteous requirement of the law might be fulfilled in us, who walk not according to the flesh but according to the Spirit. For those who live according to the flesh set their minds on the things of the*

flesh, but those who live according to the Spirit set their minds on the things of the Spirit.

When we have the *substance*, why would we go back to the *shadow*?

Imagine a young wife whose beloved husband has just returned safely from war. Can you imagine her wanting to spend her time adoring his photograph and ignoring him? She used to do that, sure, but now *he is here*. He is *present*.

Even better, our God no longer presents Himself as distant, but as near. No longer is His manifestation terrifying, but gentle. Read this contrast between Mt. Sinai (the Old Mosaic Covenant) and Mt. Zion (the New Covenant in Jesus Christ) in Hebrews 12:18-24 (emphasis mine).

> *For you have not come to what may be touched [physical things], a blazing fire and darkness and gloom and a tempest and the sound of a trumpet and a voice whose words made the hearers beg that no further messages be spoken to them.*
>
> *For they could not endure the order that was given, "If even a beast touches the mountain [Mt. Sinai, where the Law was given], it shall be stoned." Indeed, so terrifying was the sight that Moses said, "I tremble with fear."*
>
> <u>*BUT*</u> *you have come to Mount Zion and to the city of the living God, the heavenly Jerusalem, and to innumerable angels in festal gathering, and to the assembly of the firstborn who are enrolled in heaven, and to God, the judge of all, and to the spirits of the righteous made perfect, and to Jesus, the mediator of a new covenant, and to the sprinkled blood that speaks a better word than the blood of Abel.*

It's vitally important

When you grasp the truth that you can stop trying to keep the Mosaic Law and walk by the power of the Holy Spirit of Jesus Christ, it will completely transform your life.

> *But when Christ had offered for all time a single sacrifice for sins, he sat down at the right hand of God, waiting from that time until his enemies should be made a footstool for his feet. For by a single offering he has perfected for all time those who are being sanctified.*
>
> *And the Holy Spirit also bears witness to us; for after saying,*
>
> *"This is the covenant that I will make with them*
>   *after those days, declares the Lord:*
> *I will put my laws on their hearts,*
>   *and write them on their minds,"*
>
> *then he adds, "I will remember their sins and their lawless deeds no more."*
>
> *Where there is forgiveness of these, there is no longer any offering for sin.* (Hebrews 10:12-18)

As you understand it more deeply, by digging into the New Testament to see how the Lord wants us to live, you'll also see that—unlike the Old Covenant—He has provided all that we need to do it. *All that we need.*

> *His divine power has granted to us all things that pertain to life and godliness, through the knowledge of him who called us to his own glory and excellence, by which he has granted to us his precious and very great promises, so that through them you may become partakers of the divine nature, having escaped from the corruption that is in the world because of sinful desire.* (2 Peter 1:3-4)

For me, there came a time when I finally understood I didn't have to figure out which Old Covenant commands to obey, and how. I didn't have to spend time reading scholarly debates on how the Old Covenant Law applies to our lives. I could let it go. Because the Lord Jesus Christ has not only fulfilled all that law, but when we ask and seek, He will show us the new way under the New Covenant. And not only that, but when we look to Him in faith, He will also empower us to go in that way.[32]

This is good news.

It's called "the gospel."

---

[32] There is much more that can be said about New Covenant living. I often write about it on my website, heresthejoy.com, but the best place to read about it is in the New Testament.

CHAPTER 7

"Children Obey Your Parents"?

HERE'S PART OF a letter I received through my blog:

I have a long back story but to simplify for my question, I am in my early 50s, so raised my kids in the era of the home school conference you mentioned [in the blog post "'Biblical patriarchy:' Here's How you Replaced God"]. Unfortunately I idolized the "perfect" family while covering for my emotionally abusive husband. I raised 5 children and spoon-fed them a hypocritical life, all the while making sure they learned the most important Scriptures....like children obey your parents.

Anyway, God's arm was not shortened in all my shortcomings, and He allowed my family to fall apart all while He held each one of us. He took me out of Egypt and, I believe, saved my children from further harm by allowing the divorce before they all were adults.

This all comes down to one main question.....

Please untwist Ephesians 6:1-3 and Colossians 3:20 to help release children, teens, young adults, and even adults from the bondage of following a patriarchal abusive father or any sort of abusive father.

Here is my reply.

Thank you for your letter. The situations you describe sound so difficult, and yet are sadly all too common.

You mentioned abusive fathers, but I've known of several abusive mothers too, ones who have inflicted great cruelty and even sadism on their children, either in conjunction with or separately from the children's fathers. So my response will equally apply to them.

In researching for my response, I read a number of articles that said things like "of course this doesn't apply to" . . . without explaining why. So I want to do my best to take the interpretation of these passages very seriously because I know I'm writing to young adults who truly want to follow the Lord.

One important, universal rule of Biblical interpretation is . . .

Read and understand Scripture in context

The larger context of a passage of Scripture means not only the paragraph the Scripture is in, but the entire book it's in, and then God's entire written Word, especially the New Covenant, since Hebrews tells us the New Covenant is better than the Old and supersedes the Old.

Colossians is an amazing and wonderful book unfolding to us who Jesus Christ really is and why that's important. Paul starts chapter 3 with,

> *"So [considering everything I've written about in the first 2 chapters], if you have been raised with Christ, seek the things that are above, where Christ is seated at the right hand of God. Set your minds on things above, not on things on the earth. For you have died, and your life is hidden with Christ in God."* (Colossians 3:1-3)

Then Paul lays out the directives of what life will look like when Christians are living and walking in the Spirit, for the love and joy and glory of God.

Colossians 3:18-21 say,

> *Wives, submit to your husbands, as is fitting in the Lord. Husbands, love your wives, and do not be harsh with them. Children, obey your parents in everything, for this pleases the Lord. Fathers, do not provoke your children, lest they become discouraged.*

You can see what a harmonious situation this will create when it's lived out by those who love the Lord.

The book of Ephesians, written about the same time as Colossians, and with very similar themes, also follows a similar structure: The book is divided into two parts, with the first half consisting of truths about who Jesus Christ is to you, in you, and for you, and who you are in Him. The second half delivers the roadmap of what this Christian life will look like when it is lived in the Spirit of God.

At the end of chapter 5 we see instructions for Christian wives to honor and Christian husbands to love.

Then in 6:1-4,

> *Children, obey your parents in the Lord, for this is right. "Honor your father and mother" (this is the first commandment with a promise), "that it may go well with you and that you may live long in the land."*
>
> *Fathers, do not provoke your children to anger, but bring them up in the discipline and instruction of the Lord.*

Then instructions to Christian servants to obey masters. Then instructions to Christian masters to treat servants with kindness.

And then . . .

> *Finally, be strong in the Lord and in the strength of his might. Put on the whole armor of God, that you may be able to stand against the schemes of the devil. For we do not wrestle against flesh and blood, but against the rulers, against the authorities, against the cosmic powers over this present darkness, against the spiritual forces of evil in the heavenly places. Therefore take up the whole armor of God, that you may be able to withstand in the evil day, and having done all, to stand firm.* (Ephesians 6:10-13)

Then follow five more verses describing the armor of God that each Christian is exhorted to take.

I want to make sure you notice that last part of Ephesians 6, because of that command to put on the whole armor of God and be strong in the strength of the Lord. It comes right after these commands to obey.

It's only those who are able to stand on their own before God, in the power of the Holy Spirit, who can obey according to knowledge. And the only way that can be done is by understanding who you are in Christ and who Christ is—in, and to, and for you—as has been explained in the earlier parts of this epistle.

I'll be coming back later to some of these thoughts about the context. For now, here's the first question:

What if a child's parents want him to sin?

The command to obey in Colossians 3:20 appears to be universal:

> *Children, obey your parents in all things, for this is well pleasing <u>unto the Lord</u>. (KJV)*

7 – "CHILDREN OBEY YOUR PARENTS"?

But in the parallel passage in Ephesians 6:1 (and no Scripture should be taken in isolation), we can see the qualifier more clearly:

Children, obey your parents <u>in the Lord</u>, for this is right.

So what is meant by "in the Lord"? The Jamieson, Faucett, and Brown commentary will suffice as a representation of several others (Adam Clarke, John Gill, John Calvin, John Chrysostom, and others).

Commentary on Colossians 3:20.

> <u>unto the Lord</u>–The oldest manuscripts read, "IN the Lord," that is, this is acceptable to God when it is done in the Lord, namely, from the principle of faith, and as disciples in union with the Lord.[33]

Commentary on Ephesians 6:1-3.

> <u>in the Lord</u>–Both parents and children being Christians "in the Lord," expresses the element in which the obedience is to take place, and the motive to obedience. . . . This clause, "in the Lord," would suggest the due limitation of the obedience required (Acts 5:29).[34]

There are limits on the obedience required.

I know three sisters who throughout their childhood suffered severe sexual abuse at the hands of their church-going father and his friends. One of these sisters told me that when she was a child

---

[33] *Bethany Parallel Commentary on the New Testament,* Bethany House Publishers, 1983, p 1196.

[34] Ibid., p 1157. That reference in parentheses, Acts 5:29, is "We must obey God rather than men."

of 7 or so, her Sunday school teacher taught on "Children obey your parents."

After class, this little girl asked her teacher, "What if your parent wants you to do something wrong?"

What if your parent wants you to do something wrong.

How could the Sunday school teacher possibly have guessed or fathomed, back in the early 1960s, the agony and depth of darkness that lay behind this life-hanging-in-the-balance question? Who would have dreamed, in that naïve day, that such wolves prowled the corridors of their very own churches?

The Sunday school teacher gave the predictable answer, the answer I might have given as a young Sunday school teacher.

"You still need to obey. God will take care of it."

Now, of course, we know better.

Or do we? Do we know better? For me, it took several knocks upside the head to see the truth and truly know better.

But now there are articles such as one by respected blogger Tim Challies that make claims that children need to obey because nature demands it, because the law demands it, and because the gospel demands it.[35] Teachings like this fill me with indignation with their lack of understanding of the kinds of demands that abusive parents can make of their children.

In the summer of 2017, two devotional books I wrote were published, for middle- and high-schoolers, *101 Devotions for Girls* and *101 Devotions for Guys*.[36] These devotionals were taken from true accounts in the missionary books I've written, but my

---

[35] Tim Challies, "3 Reasons Children Need to Obey Their Parents," November 28, 2016 https://www.challies.com/articles/3-reasons-children-need-to-obey-their-parents/

[36] Both published by Christian Focus Publications, 2017.

emphasis was decidedly different from other children's devotionals I perused.

So many other devotionals for children emphasize obeying parents. But with scores of accounts of familial cruelty held in my heart and my head, one thing I talked about was *how to disobey authority well.*

One of the devotionals came from a twelve-year-old Ethiopian boy whose father was a witchdoctor. The boy had converted to Christ. Predictably, his father had him beaten and nearly killed for not obeying by practicing the pagan rituals.

But the boy would not obey his father, because his father was requiring him to do something evil.

The question I asked in that devotional was "How can a son honor a father who is wicked?" My hope was that non-wicked adults could use this devotional to discuss our response to wickedness. Because it is not only in Ethiopia. It is here, in our very homes and churches.

The text was Acts 5:29, a verse I believe every child should memorize. In this passage Peter and the other apostles said in response to "authorities" who had ordered them to deny Jesus, *"We must obey God rather than men."*

Even little children, 7 or 8 years old, can be taught this truth, that there is a time when it's right to disobey earthly authorities in order to obey a higher authority. There is a time when it's right to get help. Of course if an authority figure forces a child to do wrong, then the child is not culpable, but we can actively teach them that *God doesn't require them to obey a parent who is committing crimes.*

In fact we need to listen to children and protect them from criminal parents. In their Sunday school classes, in their Christian schools and homeschool co-ops, and with their other family members, they need to learn when to disobey authorities, and how to do it well.

We have many Biblical examples to show us the way. David with King Saul; Shadrach, Meshach, and Abednego with Nebuchadnezzar; Daniel did with Darius; and Jonathan with his father.

A woman I know and greatly admire, as a little child of eight or nine stamped her foot at her "authorities" (at least one of whom was a family member authority figure) and told them she would no longer participate in the utterly devilish evil they were requiring of her. My heart swelled with admiration and respect for that little child as I heard her story. When she told me she was punished in unspeakable ways for her "disobedience," I cried for the child she was and embraced her as one of the hidden heroes of the faith.

God's directives are for truly *Christian* homes, to live in harmony and joy.

Children, obey your parents *in the Lord*.

Let's not neglect to teach that truth to the little ones who are looking to us for guidance.

CHAPTER 8

"(Adult) Children Obey Your Parents"? For Adults Raised in "Biblical Patriarchy"

CHAPTER 7 ADDRESSED the need for even young children under the supervision of their parents to learn how to resist an abusive or even wicked authority honorably.

But what about controlling parents of adults, especially those whose parents espouse some form of patriarchal beliefs? And what if it seems that the parents aren't asking them to do anything that actually promotes sin? After all, checking the odometer, for example (mentioned on page 46) isn't *sin*, is it?

In these cases, some of these adults look at the "Children obey your parents" Scriptures and believe there is no Biblical justification to do anything other than comply with everything their parents command.

Here's the second part of the letter (the first part of which was at the beginning of chapter 7).

> *My oldest son is a very loving, kind, Scripture-studied man, very opposite his father, but he cannot free his mind from those Scriptures [Ephesians 6:1-3 and Colossians 3:20] as*

> there is no clarity in Scripture as to an age when you would stop obeying and ever not submit to the authority God has placed over us.
>
> Now I have recently met a family with 6 children that the father has brought up not allowing them to get a driver's license, get a job, vote, or think on their own. They are not allowed to get counsel outside of him and not allowed to interpret Scripture outside of his interpretation. They are completely broken.
>
> I, sadly, am not equipped to give Scripture to combat the "children obey" Scriptures. Please help.

Here is my reply.

What is an adult "child" to do when told to obey a parent who isn't a criminal, but is controlling?

This is what you were really asking. My heart aches to hear the bondage that these young adults are in. I know that you believe this is not what God wants, and they may wonder if perhaps it's not what God wants, but they long to understand and obey the Scriptures.

Here's something I'd like to ask you to consider. It is appropriate to apply the word "abusive" to people who regularly harm other people. As you read this chapter, I'm asking you to consider the possibility that this word might apply to the parent in question.

With that in mind, it's important to look at the words, the context, and the entire body of Scripture, especially the New Covenant, under which we live as believers in the Lord Jesus Christ.

8 – "(ADULT) CHILDREN OBEY YOUR PARENTS"?

The word child (teknon)

Aside from the meaning of "offspring," the word *teknon* carries with it an implication of *dependence that forms a strong bond*, the kind that's perfectly appropriate in childhood. This is shown in the many times the word is used in a spiritual sense, showing our dependence on our Father God (rather than an earthly father):

> *And the disciples were amazed at his words. But Jesus said to them again, "Children, how difficult it is to enter the kingdom of God!"* (Mark 10:24)

> *The Spirit himself bears witness with our spirit that we are children of God, and if children, then heirs—heirs of God and fellow heirs with Christ. . . . that the creation itself will be set free from its bondage to corruption and obtain the freedom of the glory of the children of God.* (Romans 8:16-17, 21)

> *Therefore, preparing your minds for action, and being sober-minded, set your hope fully on the grace that will be brought to you at the revelation of Jesus Christ. As obedient children, do not be conformed to the passions of your former ignorance, but as he who called you is holy, you also be holy in all your conduct.* (1 Peter 1:13-15)

> *By this it is evident who are the children of God, and who are the children of the devil: whoever does not practice righteousness is not of God, nor is the one who does not love his brother.* (1 John 3:10)

And two uses of *teknon* in Ephesians, shortly before the one about children obeying their parents:

> *Be ye therefore followers of God, as dear children; And walk in love, as Christ also hath loved us, and hath given himself*

for us an offering and a sacrifice to God for a sweet smelling savor. (Ephesians 5:1-2)

For at one time you were darkness, but now you are light in the Lord. Walk as children of light (for the fruit of light is found in all that is good and right and true). (Ephesians 5:8-9)

An important context for the word teknon

Fathers, do not provoke your children, lest they become discouraged. (Colossians 3:21)

Fathers, do not provoke your children to anger, but bring them up in the discipline and instruction of the Lord. (Ephesians 6:4)

It sounds like from what you've described in your letter, that these young adults may have become very discouraged by their provoking father, and possibly even angry (if they have any strength to be angry).

But adult children of controlling parents who want to follow the Lord could read those commands to fathers and think, "Even if he's disobeying his command, that doesn't give me liberty to disobey mine."

But what does it mean to "bring them up" in Ephesians 6:4?

That phrase in the Greek means *nurture* or *raise to maturity*, which would imply that there will come a time when *these young, dependent children become mature*. They will grow up.

There are (at least) two aspects to reaching maturity. The first is necessary for society to function. The second is necessary for the Church to function. As you consider these two things, you can prayerfully consider whether your controlling parent has created a situation that is *designed to keep you from reaching maturity.*[37]

Societal maturity

A person attains societal maturity when he's able to provide for himself—a level of self-sufficiency that allows for independence in regard to physical needs. Greater maturity comes when seriously undertaking the responsibility to provide for one's own new and separate family in various ways.

You may have been so controlled that there's been no opportunity to show you can provide for yourself and prove your societal maturity. But if you have the basic education, willingness, desire, and energy to provide for yourself, you can do it.

When you've been all these years in the home of a controlling parent, you'll need a transition period, and it might be a long one. Be gentle with yourself. You'll need to learn boundaries.[38] And since what you experienced may well fall into the category of trauma, you won't want to neglect investigating that possibility and taking necessary steps to help your mind and body heal.[39]

As you learn and grow in new ways, as you care for the deepest parts of yourself, step by step you'll be able to see your way clear to develop as a person on your own.

---

[37] A helpful article in which the author sought the truth of these verses in Scripture can be found at http://www.recoveringgrace.org/2011/10/once-a-child-always-a-child/

[38] A helpful book for this is *Boundaries: When to Say Yes, How to Say No to Take Control of Your Life,* by Dr. Henry Cloud and Dr. John Townsend. Zondervan, 2017.

[39] Understanding the symptoms of post-traumatic stress disorder (PTSD) can help you get direction. A helpful book on this subject is *The Body Keeps the Score: Brain, Mind, and Body in the Healing of Trauma,* by Bessel van der Kolk M.D. Penguin Books, 2015.

Spiritual maturity

A person attains the most basic level of spiritual maturity when he or she depends on the Lord Jesus Christ instead of on another person for the personal relationship with God. Greater maturity comes as the Christian increases in experiential knowledge of God and wisdom regarding His ways, and as love for God and others increases.

God's assignment to parents is to raise their children *to maturity*. Continuing to exert coercive control is the opposite of that, working to prevent their children's true adulthood. At the extreme, it may even actively attempt to stamp out their personhood.

The context of Ephesians and Colossians

All the commands for specific relationships in Ephesians and Colossians are given in a specific context. That context is the overarching pattern for relating taught by the entire New Testament: the practice of "one anothering."

Beginning with Jesus' new command to "love one another" (John 13:34-35), the New Testament repeatedly admonishes us to honor one another, teach one another, serve one another, submit to one another, admonish one another, live in harmony with one another, and more. (See, for example, Mark 9:50, Romans 12:10, Galatians 5:13, Ephesians 4:2, Colossians 3:13, 1 Thessalonians 4:18, Hebrews 3:13, James 5:16, 1 Peter 3:8, 1 John 3:11, 23.)

That is, in our "horizontal" relationships in Christ—especially adult-to-adult relationships—these "one anothers" naturally flow back and forth. These "one another" commands preclude one attitude or action (like admonishing) going only one way in the relationship while another attitude or action (like submitting) goes only the other way.

8 – "(ADULT) CHILDREN OBEY YOUR PARENTS"?

The word obey

The Greek word *hupakouo* means "to listen attentively in order to respond appropriately." But it doesn't have any necessary implications about what that response will actually be.

Sometimes this word is used in exactly the way we would think, of immediate compliance with a command. This is the way it's used, for example, of the demons obeying Jesus in the gospels and of our Lord Jesus' willingness to die for us.[40]

But it's also the same word used when Rhoda came to the door where Peter was knocking after he had gotten out of prison in Acts 12. Even though she didn't open the door, she did actually "listen attentively" at the door.

"Obedience" doesn't mean giving over your mind and will to be controlled by another person.

For example, consider the case in which your parent is telling you what to do, without telling you directly to sin. As a thinking adult you may still be able to observe that some aspect of the family dynamics is enabling or even increasing sin in the parent's own life (and this is where you might be told to "be content" as is described in chapter 11). In this case, "listening attentively" could mean that you prayerfully decide to respectfully refuse to follow the instructions you've been given.

"Listening attentively" implies a respectful attitude. But as noted in chapter 7, even young children need not exercise mindless acquiescence. *If they stand against wrongdoing in their authorities, this will reflect the heart of God.*

The same is true for adults, and even more so.

In a healthy home, as the child grows into maturity there will be a gradual shift from obedience as "listening attentively in

---

[40] Romans 5:19. "For as by the one man's disobedience the many were made sinners, so by the one man's obedience the many will be made righteous."

order to do what I'm told" to obedience as "listening attentively, but having some leeway to decide for myself how to respond appropriately."

Over time, this second response will more and more include the adult-to-adult embracing of "submitting to one another out of reverence for Christ" (Ephesians 5:21).

The context of the rest of the Bible

Just as the command "children obey your parents" should be considered in the context of the immediate Scripture, so should it be considered in the wider context of the entire Word of God, especially as we consider especially the "one anothering" commands that the New Testament teaches as the basis for all adult-to-adult relationships in Christ.

If they are adults trusting in Jesus, then the descriptions and commands for adult Christians throughout the epistles apply to them.

This brings me to the most disturbing part of your letter. The six young adult children are not allowed to think on their own. They are not allowed to interpret Scripture outside the father's interpretation.

These adults are not allowed to read the Bible and ask the Holy Spirit to enlighten their understanding and draw their own conclusions about anything in the Word of God.

These adults are not allowed to think.

It is this thought control, more than anything else, that ultimately causes this situation to become more like a concentration camp than a family.

So here's my Biblical counsel to these adults . . .

. . . based on Scriptures that I'll lay out. This counsel applies equally to adult daughters as it does to adult sons, because the New Covenant draws no distinction between men and women regarding these points.

Begin thinking on your own

But not just on your own, really, but begin prayerfully studying the Word of God, asking the Holy Spirit to open your eyes to it, so you can see and know who Jesus really is.

You might want to begin with the gospels to see who Jesus really is, but at some point I'd suggest studying Colossians and Ephesians, the books that contain the commands you asked about.

If your father forbids you from studying on your own lest you come to conclusions that differ from his, study anyway, in secret, because you are a child of God, and God has called you to know Him and be known by Him.

And you must obey God rather than man.

Listen to His voice

Jesus said in John 10:27, "My sheep hear My voice, and I know them, and they follow me."

As you're in the Scriptures and getting to know the Lord Jesus Christ—truly know Him—you will be strengthened in your inner man, your core. More and more, as one of His sheep you'll know your Shepherd's voice.

Be willing to hear from God, even if He might tell you something different from what your parent has said. Throughout His Word He has called you to Himself.

He will give you the fortitude you need to do what He calls you to do. It's a matter of whose voice you're going to "attentively listen" to.

Jesus said be willing to forsake father and mother to follow Him

In Matthew 19:29, Mark 10:29-30, Luke 14:26, and Luke 18:29-30, the words of our Lord Jesus are recorded as telling us to forsake parents in order to follow Him. If you think, "But obeying my parents *is* the way I follow Christ," then I challenge you to stand up and be the adult God has called you to be and get the mediator out from between you.

There is only one Mediator

First Timothy 2:5 tells us there is only one mediator between God and man, and that is Jesus Christ, not any man or woman. Jesus is the only one. He is the one who has torn open the temple curtain for you, *you yourself,* to enter the holiest place of all, the very presence of God, as Hebrews 4:16 says, and obtain mercy and find grace to help in time of need.

This "grace to help"—He'll help you do the right thing in following God instead of man. I talked in my "idol factory" blog post[41] about appeasement of a false god, which may be what you've been doing without even realizing it.

---

[41] "Rethinking the idol factory: challenging the 'idol' construct as the explanation for all sin in the lives of Christians." https://www.heresthejoy.com/2017/01/rethinking-the-idol-factory-challenging-the-idol-construct-as-the-explanation-for-all-sin-in-the-lives-of-christians/

Search the Scriptures to see Him

If you're afraid, know how tender and compassionate our Lord Jesus is with those who are afraid. "Fear not little flock," He said to His fearful disciples in Luke 12:32, "for it is the Father's good pleasure to give you the kingdom." Look to Him to give you the courage you need for the full-fledged Christian life. He has called you to it.

Cry out to Him to show Himself to you, through His Word, through His Spirit, for your filling, and for His glory.

Find out, for example, what Paul meant in the book of Colossians (the same book with one of those commands) when he said in 2:6-10,

> *Therefore, as you received Christ Jesus the Lord, so walk in him, rooted and built up in him and established in the faith, just as you were taught, abounding in thanksgiving. See to it that no one takes you captive by philosophy and empty deceit, according to human tradition, according to the elemental spirits of the world, and not according to Christ. For in him the whole fullness of deity dwells bodily, and you have been filled in him, who is the head of all rule and authority.*

Acknowledge Him as your supreme Authority

As an adult Christian, one who is willing to forsake your father and mother to follow Jesus Christ (Luke 14:26), you look to Him alone for all your salvation, not to anyone else.

There is much life to be lived in the power of the one who has all authority in heaven and on earth. "All authority is given unto Me in heaven and on earth," says our Lord Jesus Christ. (Matthew 28:18) He is the Authority you must seek and follow.

Come to Him for rest and water

Our Lord Jesus Christ says to you, "Come to me!"

> *Come to me, all who labor and are heavy laden, and I will give you rest. Take my yoke upon you, and learn from me, for I am gentle and lowly in heart, and you will find rest for your souls. For my yoke is easy, and my burden is light.* (Matthew 11:28-30)

I'm guessing you may have felt heavy laden, and the rest He promises may have felt distant.

I'm telling you it's here, and it's available for you.

> *On the last day of the feast, the great day, Jesus stood up and cried out, "If anyone thirsts, let him come to me and drink. Whoever believes in me, as the Scripture has said, 'Out of his heart will flow rivers of living water.'" Now this he said about the Spirit, whom those who believed in him were to receive.* (John 7:37-39)

This is the theme passage for my website, Here's the Joy. Jesus calls you—you, without anyone else in between—to come to Him and drink of the living, sparkling, flowing waters He offers you through the Holy Spirit, Christ in you, the hope of glory. Are you thirsty for that?

Become a Kingdom warrior

Our Lord Jesus Christ, the Captain of the Host of the Lord, has called you to wear the armor of God in Ephesians 6. That's the passage that comes right after the commands to obey.

That is for you, as a mature adult in Jesus Christ, standing on your own two feet in the righteousness of Jesus Christ. You are called to take the helmet of the salvation provided in Jesus Christ, the breastplate of the righteousness of Jesus Christ, the shoes of the preparation of the gospel of peace found in Jesus Christ. You are called to gird your loins about with the truth of Jesus Christ and wield the sword of the Spirit, which is the Living Word of God, Jesus Christ. You are called to hold the shield of faith, by which you will quench the fiery darts of the wicked.

You are called to stand up and be a faithful warrior in the Kingdom of God.

You are no longer a child, dependent on someone else for your relationship with Jesus Christ. You can know Him personally, intimately. You can know Him.

And if He calls you to go . . . you can follow Him.

The most important word of wisdom anyone could give you is this: seek Jesus Christ through His Word, all of His Word but especially the New Testament that reveals Him clearly (not in shadow, as does the Old Testament). Seek to understand what His death and resurrection—which aren't talked about much in "Biblical patriarchy," from what I understand—apply to your everyday life.

Ask God to open your eyes and show you what He's saying, and rely on His Holy Spirit to teach you. Don't be afraid to talk about what you're learning in the Scriptures, and ask questions about what you're trying to understand.

Refuse to take "you're just a woman/child/teenager/single person so you don't need to think about that" (or any of its variants) for an answer. When you stand before God one day, that's an answer that will be unacceptable to Him.

I'm praying for you . . .

. . . that the God of our Lord Jesus Christ, the Father of glory,

may give you the Spirit of wisdom and of revelation in the knowledge of him,

having the eyes of your hearts enlightened,

that you may know what is the hope to which he has called you,

what are the riches of his glorious inheritance in the saints,

and what is the immeasurable greatness of his power toward us who believe,

according to the working of his great might that he worked in Christ when he raised him from the dead and seated him at his right hand in the heavenly places,

far above all rule and authority and power and dominion, and above every name that is named, not only in this age but also in the one to come.

(That's from Ephesians too.)

There is so much life to be lived,[42] in the power of God the Spirit, for the joy of knowing our Lord and Savior and being known by Him, experiencing His love and reaching out to others who need that Living Water.

I pray that our loving God will heal you and strengthen you and empower you for this great adventure.[43]

---

[42] I want to add that when I say "there is much life to be lived," I'm not talking about jumping into fleshly indulgences, not at all. That is a way of death. I long to see young adults walking in the light of Jesus Christ and listening to His voice and living for Him, not in rebellion to Him with all kinds of wanton sins. However, the people who write to me aren't the ones who want to live a wanton lifestyle. They're the ones who want to follow Jesus but feel, or have felt, stuck and nearly hopeless.

[43] Some significant discussion took place in the comments on my blog post of this article, including questions and answers about Scriptures, which have now been compiled into Appendix B.

CHAPTER 9

The King, the Prisoner, the Soldier, and Jesus (Bill Gothard's Teachings on Authority)

A WOMAN OFF-HANDEDLY said to me that Bill Gothard—the founder of the Institute in Basic Life Principles[44] and the Advanced Training Institute for homeschooling families[45]—is now passé because "no one listens to him anymore."

But this is incorrect. Even though the number of Gothard's avid followers is shrinking, his organizations continue to operate with the same harmful materials as ever.

Also, and perhaps more important, we can't overestimate the vast influence of Bill Gothard over the conservative Christian world. Like other teachings through the ages, many of the most significant core beliefs have held even after the scaffolding has broken down.

---

[44] https://iblp.org
[45] https://atii.org

When I was researching for the first *Untwisting Scriptures* book, about surrendering your rights, Biblical bitterness, and taking up offenses,[46] I saw that Bill Gothard's influence is starkly evident even in more mainstream teachings.

Another reason it's important to address Gothard's teachings head-on is that there are many from his abusive system who are seeking counseling now. They're trying to explain to their counselors what they experienced.

In his Basic Life Principles seminar, Gothard addresses his crucial principle of "authority" in Session 4, "How to Relate to 4 Authorities," and Session 5, "How to Make a Wise Appeal."

His four authorities are parents (mainly fathers), government, church, and business. This book you're reading now addresses the parents and the church.

From my very own Institute in Basic Youth Conflicts seminar notebook,[47] Gothard gives three main purposes for being "under authority":

1. *To grow in wisdom and character.* For this, his example is Jesus in Luke 2:52. "And Jesus increased in wisdom and in stature and in favor with God and man."
2. *To gain protection from destructive temptations.* For this, his (negative) example is King Saul in 1 Samuel 15:23a. "For rebellion is as the sin of witchcraft."
3. *To receive clear direction for life decisions.* For this, his examples are Daniel, who went through the laborious process of "making a wise appeal" to his authority, in Daniel 1 and the centurion in Matthew 8:9, who apparently received clear

---

[46] Rebecca Davis, *Untwisting Scriptures that were used to tie you up, gag you, and tangle your mind.* Justice Keepers Publishing, 2016.

[47] *Institute in Basic Youth Conflicts seminar notebook*, "Authority and Responsibility" section, p 1. IBYC publishers, 1975.

direction for life decisions when he asked Jesus to heal his servant.

Jesus: growing in wisdom and character

In Session 5, "How to Make a Wise Appeal," Gothard says,

> *If you want to follow Jesus, he got the calling when he was 12, and he said I must be about my father's business, but his parents didn't go along with the idea, and here the Son of God got under his parents' authority and when he did, he grew in wisdom and stature and favor with God and man until he was 30 years old. And he was able to accomplish a whole lot more from 30 on because he obeyed the father in all aspects.*[48]

Never mind the fact that when I was sitting under Bill Gothard I took notes furiously and believed everything he was telling me. This teaching is astonishing in its falsehood.

Here is the full story. Twelve-year-old Jesus stayed behind in the temple at Jerusalem to talk with the teachers there, while his parents headed home in the crowd. They realized He wasn't with them and came back to find Him.

> *After three days they found him in the temple, sitting among the teachers, listening to them and asking them questions. And all who heard him were amazed at his understanding and his answers. And when his parents saw him, they were astonished. And his mother said to him, "Son, why have you treated us so? Behold, your father and I have been searching for you in great distress." And he said to*

---

[48] Basic Life Principles Seminar 1985, Session 5 "How to Make a Wise Appeal," https://embassymedia.com/media/session-05-how-make-wise-appeal

> them, "Why were you looking for me? Did you not know that I must be in my Father's house?" And they did not understand the saying that he spoke to them. And he went down with them and came to Nazareth and was submissive to them. And his mother treasured up all these things in her heart. And Jesus increased in wisdom and in stature and in favor with God and man. (Luke 2:46-52)

First of all, do you notice that the Son of God rebuked His parents?

A twelve-year-old boy rebuked his parents. And yet Gothard glossed over that and ignored it.

Secondly, it wasn't that His parents "didn't go along with the idea," as Gothard said. They didn't understand it. That is a huge difference. From verse 51, though, we see that Mary "treasured all these things in her heart," as she had when the shepherds first came at the birth of her son, back in verse 19.

She had a heart inclined toward God, and she wanted to understand.

And finally, there is no correlation except in Gothard's imagination, that the growth of Jesus in verse 52 happened because of his obedience to His parents.

Jesus grew physically. Was that because of His obedience to His parents? No, that was the natural process of human growth.

Jesus grew in wisdom. Was that because of His obedience to His parents? Gothard would certainly have you think so. But look back and see. Look back at those Scriptures that describe young Jesus at twelve years old, when according to Gothard He wasn't submitting to his parents the way He should have. Even at that time He was already so wise that He caused the teachers to be amazed. That was the point from which he was growing, not because of His obedience to His parents.

Jesus grew in favor with God. Was this through His obedience to His parents? No, Jesus had a relationship with the Father unlike any other, since He was in fact the Son of God. Even if He had been an orphan, He would have grown in favor with God.

Jesus grew in favor with those around Him. This is the one point at which I would say, "Yes, His relationship with His (God-honoring) parents, in the Lord, is part of this."

But Gothard is trying to make "obedience to parents" the basis of Jesus "growing in wisdom and character." This is simply untrue.

King Saul: rebellion, the sin like witchcraft

King Saul, along with his rebellion like witchcraft, gets his own chapter, chapter 10.

Daniel: making a wise appeal

Gothard goes into great detail with the example of Daniel, using him as an example of what the norm should be between underlings and overlings.

But Daniel was a prisoner.

I actually agree that these six things based on Gothard's plan for a wise appeal[49] can be good things. (I've changed the wording slightly to make them more accurate to truth.)

1. Have a good attitude.
2. Have a clear conscience.
3. Discern the basic intentions of the person in "authority" over us.
4. Offer creative alternatives when possible.

---

[49] *Institute in Basic Youth Conflicts seminar notebook*, "Authority and Responsibility" section, pp 15-16. IBYC, 1975.

5. Make appeals when appropriate.
6. Pray for God to change a (wise) authority's mind and heart.

And without a doubt in this life, Christians may

7. Suffer for refusing to do what is wrong.

One problem with using Daniel as our example for "making a wise appeal" is that we should not have to approach those in a position of "authority" with a sense that our lives are in danger. We should be able to actually have a discussion with them.[50] When we are both adults, we should be able to discuss with them as equals.

A young person or adult shouldn't have to live in fear that they haven't done all the six things. And actually, because these things are good to do, they are good for *all* Christians to do, not only those "under authority." All Christians should have a good attitude, have a clear conscience, try to discern the basic intentions of the other person with whom they disagree, offer creative alternatives, make appeals, and pray for God to change the other person's heart and mind to be aligned with God's will. All Christians should be willing to suffer for doing what is right.

This example is flawed. As I said to a commenter on my blog, who used both Daniel and Joseph as examples of how young people should act toward their parents,

> *I'm sorry to see you compare the situations of young women in Christian families to the situations of Daniel and Joseph, both of whom were prisoners. The Christian home should not be modeled after a prison system, and Christian young women shouldn't be kept prisoners, as far too many of them*

---

[50] Abraham had a discussion with the Lord about the impending destruction of Sodom without first going through these steps. He trusted the Lord to do right.

are.[51]

Gothard said that Daniel needed to be "under the king's authority" in order to "receive clear direction for life's decisions." But how far from the truth this is!

Instead, the clear truth is that Daniel humbly challenged the king's edict because God had already given him clear direction for his decisions. He knew his life was in danger when he challenged the king, but he knew what he needed to do. The steps he took were simply finding the safest way to do it.

The centurion: "being under" authority

By far the primary Gothardian example of how important it is for us to be "under authority" is the story of the centurion, found in Matthew 8:5-10.

> *When he had entered Capernaum, a centurion came forward to him, appealing to him, "Lord, my servant is lying paralyzed at home, suffering terribly." And he said to him, "I will come and heal him." But the centurion replied, "Lord, I am not worthy to have you come under my roof, but only say the word, and my servant will be healed. For I too am a man under authority, with soldiers under me. And I say to one, 'Go,' and he goes, and to another, 'Come,' and he comes, and to my servant, 'Do this,' and he does it." When Jesus heard this, he marveled and said to those who followed him, "Truly, I tell you, with no one in Israel have I found such faith."*

---

[51] Comment on "For shame, beautiful Botkins" https://her-esthejoy.com/2013/12/for-shame-beautiful-botkins/

Gothard told this story at the beginning of Basic Seminar Session 5 and then asked, "What did that centurion have in the way of faith that no one else in Israel had?"[52]

You might think that the answer would be that he understood the power and authority of Jesus Christ, as apparently the disciples did not when they feared they were going to die in the storm.

But according to Gothard, you would be so wrong. No, Gothard said,

He understood the chain of command.[53]

Here's me in my honesty. When I was in my early twenties, and perhaps beyond, I really studied this section of Gothard's red notebook, over and over, because I did *not* understand how the story of the centurion taught the chain of command. I figured my lack of ability to grasp it was because of my dense brain, and if I just studied it enough, I would get it.

Here was that centurion living in a chain of command. Here was the emperor and the general and the captain and the cohort and different ones down the line. If the general wanted something done, he didn't go out and do it, he just gave the word. And as he gave the word, the appropriate one down the line carried it out.[54]

So . . . I thought. It's not about having faith in Jesus, really. It's about understanding how the chain of command works. God the Father is the authority, and Jesus is under Him, and then we're

---

[52] Basic Life Principles Seminar, Session 5 "How to Make a Wise Appeal," https://embassymedia.com/media/session-05-how-make-wise-appeal

[53] Ibid.

[54] Ibid.

9 – BILL GOTHARD'S TEACHINGS ABOUT AUTHORITY

under Jesus, kind of. And the centurion was in a chain of command too, in the army, yes, I see that. . . .

And Gothard twists it all to show us with his sweet smile that the way we grow in faith, to be like the centurion, the man of great faith, is NOT about believing in the Lord Jesus Christ.

No. It is about "getting under authority."

I would laugh now, if this weren't so serious and hadn't destroyed so many lives. As a commenter at Recovering Grace said,

> *If the Gospel's point was chain-of-command authority, why wasn't the Centurion advised to seek help and guidance from his Tribune, Legion Commander or Roman Governor rather than bypass his earthly authorities and go straight to the Son of God who was NOT recognized by the Centurion's authority structure?*[55]

Gothard even goes so far as to quote Hebrews 11:6, "without faith it is impossible to please God" in his twisting.

But what faith is Hebrews 11:6 actually talking about? Faith in an earthly chain of command? No. It is *faith in the living Son of God, Jesus Christ.*

In all actuality, the centurion's faith wasn't about faith in the chain of command. His faith was in the mighty Son of God.

Now that I've had more years to understand the Scriptures, here is another way to say what the centurion said.

> *"Lord, I know You have power. I have a certain amount of power vested in me too, so I get how that works. I can tell people to go and come and they'll do it. So I know that You, having all power in heaven and earth, have power over storms and diseases just the way you do over everything*

---

[55] Comment by Don Rubottom at https://www.recoveringgrace.org/2014/09/is-jesus-a-sinner-according-to-bill-gothards-teachings/

else. If you tell them to go, they'll go. You only have to say the word."

This showed an understanding of who Jesus was and what He could do. *That* is true faith.

True faith in the authority of the Lord Jesus Christ even over disease—that's what this story is about.

Bill Gothard deflected this worship, this homage, this true faith that the centurion was showing to the Lord of creation, and made it be about human beings. [56]

Gothard had told us that the centurion's "great faith" in "being under [human] authority" helped him "receive clear direction for life decisions." But, like the Daniel story, we see that this conclusion bears no relation to the story, or reality, at all.

Ultimately, we see that Gothard has wrenched and twisted a Scripture completely out of context in a way that ends up promoting human idolatry. And those teachers who follow in his footsteps do the same.

---

[56] Gothard may have been influenced by the book *Spiritual Authority*, by Watchman Nee, published in 1972 by Christian Fellowship Publishers. On page 20 of that book, Nee writes, "A beloved servant of a centurion was sick. The centurion knew he was both under authority and in authority over others. So he asked the Lord to say a word, believing the work of healing would thus be done—for are not all authorities in the Lord's hand? He believed in the Lord's authority. No wonder our Lord commended him for his great faith." You might think from reading this that Nee wanted to emphasize the Lord's authority over the illness, but this is just a small statement in the midst of a book about submitting to human authorities. About this Nee says, "Today the universe is full of authorities set up by God." (page 22)

Chapter 10

Rebellion is the Sin like Witchcraft

I RECEIVED THIS comment on my blog regarding living as an adult child in a patriarchal home:

> *We can study the scriptures on our own and come to conclusions, and [our father] can't stop us; however when those conclusions lead us to take action against what he desires, now we are sinning and in rebellion against him and God.*
>
> *He presents a very convincing argument and at the end of every conversation [we feel] confusion and doubt...*

This comment alludes to a Scripture that has been held over the heads of those who want to get safe or help get others safe. First Samuel 15:23a says,

> *For rebellion is as the sin of witchcraft.*

That is one scary Scripture!

The context

So, we are taught in some Christian circles, "When your authority, especially a Christian authority, tells you to do something, if you don't obey, you are guilty of being in rebellion against God. And rebellion is as the sin of witchcraft, so you will be condemned by God."

This is especially used by parents who want to maintain control over their adult children and by church leaders who want unquestioning obedience from their people.

> *"We were taught that 'Rebellion is as the sin of witchcraft' (Samuel 15:23) in that like witchcraft, rebellion puts you in 'Satan's realm.' The fear this created in women and teens just looking to assert their own decisions is hard to explain. Illustrations about teens in cars listening to (forbidden by parents) rock music, traveling to be with friends or other places that their parents disapproved of being killed in cars (clearly God's judgement) and other similar examples, were prolific. The story of Jacob's daughter, Dinah, was then provided as the knockout punch."*[57]

Of course for these leaders it's super important to make sure the people who hear this scary Bible verse never get the context.

So let's talk about that.

The context here is that King Saul had received a word *directly from God Himself,* from the only source of messages from God at that time (the voice of the prophet), and he had *directly* defied it.

That is the context. Rebellion is defined here as *direct* defiance against God's *direct* word.

---

[57] Comment by DSwank on "Spiritual Umbrellas and the Oppression of Women" at https://timfall.com/2017/02/22/spiritual-umbrellas-suppress-women

Gothard's teaching

In his teaching about King Saul, Gothard says,

> *"Scripture records that on three major occasions King Saul rebelled against the word of the Lord, and on each occasion there was a specific consequence."* [58]

Yes, Saul lived a sad and rebellious life with serious consequences. But again, this rebellion was against God directly rather than refusing to go along with the commands of any authority between him and God.

If Moses' parents had ever thought, "Well, God put this authority of Pharaoh over us, so we'd better obey him and just trust God to protect our little one," they would never have taken the drastic action that they did to keep their baby safe, trusting Moses to the dangers of the Nile River rather than the dangers of a ruler who had dedicated his life to evil.

If Joseph, the husband of Mary, had thought, "This king is the one put in authority over me, so I'd better obey him and trust God to keep baby Jesus safe," he wouldn't have listened to the dream warning and taken action.

In the Basic Life Principles seminar, which thousands upon thousands and hundreds of thousands of Christians attended and were deeply influenced by over the years, Bill Gothard explained to young people that they should be under their parents' authority. Then with his gentle humor he added,

> *But Bill you don't understand. My parents aren't Christians. In fact, I think they're possessed by evil spirits.* [59]

---

[58] *Institute in Basic Youth Conflicts seminar notebook*, "Authority and Responsibility" section, p 9. IBYC publishers, 1975.

[59] Basic Life Principles Seminar, Session 5 "How to Make a Wise Appeal," https://embassymedia.com/media/session-05-how-make-wise-appeal

Bill gave a little smile. The audience guffawed.

Friends, I remember laughing heartily at this.

Utterly ridiculous, of course. Utterly ridiculous to think that anyone's parents could ever be demonized.

And what about David when he was interacting with Saul—the very one who was accused of rebellion? Yes, well, what do you know, he was troubled by an evil spirit (1 Samuel 16:14). That is, by definition, he was demonized.[60]

Not only was Saul David's king, but he also became his father-in-law. So in Gothard's way of thinking, he was David's authority twice over.

But David disobeyed the king's command to stay in the king's house, he disobeyed the king's command to come to the king's dinner. Instead he hid in the mountains. *For years.*

Bill Gothard, though, in his efforts to get us to agree with his "authority" teachings, twists these Scriptures. He does indeed acknowledge that David's father-in-law and king was afflicted by an evil spirit. But then he says,

> *And David had to flee for his life, and yet God gives us the heart of David. He said, "I will not lift up my hand against the Lord's anointed."*[61]

So if we stop and think about this a bit, we'll see that Gothard is admitting that the only thing David determined to do was not kill the king.

---

[60] See page 171 for a fuller definition of "demonization."

[61] Basic Life Principles Seminar, Session 4 "How to Relate to Four Authorities," https://embassymedia.com/media/session-04-how-relate-four-authorities

I also encourage all those who are under abusive authorities to refrain from killing those authorities. So he and I can agree on that.

Even Gothard himself admits—glossing over it, yes, but admits—that David *fled* from a demonized authority.

Of course he never pointed out—because it would be antithetical to his purposes—that David was blessed by God when he fled from that authority.

How to know if you're rebelling

I know of several families in which older siblings who have escaped have eventually been able to help younger siblings escape, because yes, the control, abuse, and even outright wickedness is that bad. All the threats of "you're not honoring your parents, you rebellious children" and "God will punish you for this" are laid aside as the adult children have honored abusive parents the best they can by refusing to interact with them.

They learn that as adults they can honor their parents without obeying them. And they are doing what they can to help keep other safe from harm.

So what does that Scripture, 1 Samuel 15:23a, actually mean?

First of all, witchcraft involves getting in touch with the spirit world in a way that ignores and even defies the authority and Lordship of God Himself. We should rightly tremble to think that rebellion is actually similar.

But it is rebellion *against the Lord Himself* that is being described here. Rebellion against the Lord Himself does ignore and even defy His authority. So yes, in that way it is similar to witchcraft.

But this accusation has been hurled at His true people, who only want to love, serve, and obey Him with all their hearts.

If that is your heart toward Him, then you're not in rebellion. You may have some confusion (from twisted Scriptures), but you're not in rebellion.

If your heart is to follow the Lord Jesus Christ, to know Him and to love Him, you can be relieved of this accusation. You are not in rebellion. You can be truly encouraged on your journey.

CHAPTER 11

"You Just Need to Be Content"

IN AN ARTICLE called "Destroy Her with Discontent," Desiring God tells us that "discontent" is Satan's trap against every woman.[62] In the style of *Screwtape Letters*, author Rebekah Wilson Merkle offers "advice" from one demon to another. Here is a sampling:

> *Keep them looking at their husband's failings ("he just doesn't seem to even care about my needs") and not their own heart. . . .*
>
> *If it happens that you can't keep them from the book [the Bible] completely . . . keep all their thoughts focused on how their husband isn't living up to the instructions the book contains. . . .*
>
> *You want to encourage friendships that will feed and pet the discontent, rather than uproot it. Even prayer groups and mentorships are fabulous places for this to happen. . . .*

---

[62] Rebekah Wilson Merkle, "Destroy Her with Discontent: Satan's Aim for Every Woman." https://www.desiringgod.org/articles/destroy-her-with-discontent, July 22, 2017.

I wrote a response explaining how telling readers to be "content" in every relationship can serve to keep a woman and her children in a highly abusive situation.

For example, "he doesn't seem to even care about my needs" could apply to the story I heard from a woman who was swarmed by yellow jackets while her husband got in the car and drove away, laughing.

Telling her mentors and prayer group friends that he's not "living up to the instructions the book contains" could apply to the wife whose husband is living a double life filled with adultery.

But then a woman wrote to me with a response of her own. Since she grew up under "Biblical Patriarchy," her response is important here. The following are her words.

The response by the guest writer

When I lived at home with my parents, I used to write articles about contentment and joy. I saw that they were closely connected in the Scripture, and I desired to live out those characteristics of a Christian's life. My father would often tell me that he was grateful for my contented, joyful spirit. He would proofread much of my writing and he agreed that I could say such things because they were true of my life.

The years passed, and I began questioning the negative patterns, sinful behaviors, wrong attitudes, and hurtful actions of my parents toward others.

Suddenly I was accused of being discontent. My questions were never answered; the responsibility to "have the right attitude" was put on my shoulders. I was constantly told that if I continued to raise questions about serious issues in my family, I was being discontent and unsubmissive. So I began to study the sin of discontent in God's Word with an open heart.

11 – "YOU JUST NEED TO BE CONTENT"

My study led me to understand that true contentment means to be at rest, characterized by peace and deep-rooted joy with the purposes of God. It is a satisfaction that God knows the needs of His children.

To be content is to be controlled by the power of the Holy Spirit in each circumstance, trial, or hardship.

But contentment does not mean *resignation to or agreement with sinful practices*. Contentment does not mean *complacency or willful ignorance*.

The conclusion I reached was that I was not discontent with God's provision in my life. I always had everything I needed, and I was not pining away wanting things I did not have. I did not complain about wanting more than what I was given. I was actually quite content and grateful to the Lord for His provision in my life.

My response to my parents was, "I have searched and studied the Scriptures, and I've asked God to show me my heart. I've asked Him to reveal truth." I shared my heart with my parents, what I had discovered in God's Word, my own satisfaction with what God had given to me, how I didn't yearn after more things or complain about circumstances. I was transparent about my heart's attitude.

However, after careful study of God's Word, I did recognize that there was something I should be "discontent" about. Sin. No Christian should ever be satisfied, accepting, or tolerant of the habitual sinning of others, especially if those sins are harming people.

I shared with my parents that I was "discontent" with the sin in my family. Carefully and specifically, I stated the areas of direct disobedience to the Word of God that were occurring in the family. It wasn't about a frustration with petty offenses or annoyances (such as dirty socks on the floor). The sins that I confronted were pornography, slander, vitriolic anger, malicious speech, control and manipulation, hypocrisy, and idolatry.

Over the years, I've heard much teaching on the sin of discontent, and it often focuses mainly on letting go of petty grievances. But that falls into the category of forbearance, not contentment.

In recent years, I've also noticed that those who are being severely abused and who question that abuse are charged with learning to be more content. "Suck it up and trust God with your trial. You need to learn contentment."

This is an unloving response to those who are in harm's way, trapped, afraid, and desperate for life and freedom.

Distinguish discontent from non-sins

I appreciate this writer's thoughts. With material like Rebekah Wilson Merkle's article from trusted sources such as Desiring God, abusers will have more fodder to accuse their victims of "discontent."

But what's more, these accusations will come even from well-meaning people in the church who haven't taken the time to study and find out what contentment really is, and with what circumstances we should never be "content."

It is important for us as Christians to distinguish between, on the one hand

- *the Christian principle of "contentment with necessary provisions" (see for example 1 Timothy 6:8) and the forbearance that Christians are to practice with human foibles*

from, on the other hand

- *a complacent acquiescence that refrains from acknowledging and confronting obvious sin.*

11 – "YOU JUST NEED TO BE CONTENT"

No such distinction was made in their article. The implication instead was that any negative word about a woman's relationship was an evidence of her "discontent."

How essential it is for us as the church of Jesus Christ to extend the hand to women or young people who may sound "discontent" and to *listen* to them.

They may in fact be struggling to come to terms with reality, facing off with wickedness they may have previously been unable or unwilling to admit.

This, after all, is not "discontent." This is living in integrity. And for the church, it's one more opportunity to defend and show compassion to the downtrodden.

PART THREE

The Problem of Church "Authorities"

CHAPTER 12

The Umbrella Heresy—at Home and Church

THE UMBRELLA HERESY (whether or not your particular version of it used an umbrella) teaches that the one in a position of authority over you is a spiritual covering and protection for you.

It's hard to "untwist Scriptures" about a ubiquitous teaching in evangelicalism that isn't even based on any Scriptures at all.

Never anywhere in the Bible, never are we told anything about *anyone having a position of authority that becomes a spiritual covering for anyone else.*

But that hasn't stopped these teachers.

What Bill Gothard himself actually still says

Here's what Gothard still says, as of the writing of this book:

> *As long as a person is under an umbrella, he finds shelter from harsh weather conditions. If he steps out from under the umbrella, he exposes himself to the environment. . . .*
>
> *By honoring and submitting to authorities, you will*

> *receive the privileges of their protection, direction, and accountability. If you resist their instructions and move out from their jurisdictional care, you forfeit your place under their protection and face life's challenges and temptations on your own.*[63]

Of course, for anyone who actually knows the Bible (which I didn't in the 1970s and 1980s when I was in my teens and twenties devouring this teaching) the natural response would be . . .

You just made that up.

There is no Biblical basis for it, and there is much Biblical evidence against it. But Gothard, who claims to be an evangelical Christian, didn't let that stop him.

At first Gothard called this concept the *"chain of command"*—that's what it is in my old books from the 1970s. This is where he used the centurion as an example of a "man under authority" (to buttress his "chain of command" ideas instead of showing him to be an example of great faith in the power and authority of the Lord Jesus Christ, as the Bible does, all of which is addressed earlier, in Chapter 9).

Later he changed the name to the *"umbrella of authority."* I'm guessing it was because he wanted to withdraw a bit from terminology that sounded so military, but I don't know that for sure.

Then in later years this same concept became the *"umbrella of protection"* so it could sound really nice. Good PR move.

In order to help indoctrinate all those with their eyes on the prize in this teaching (which is not only nowhere in the Bible but is actually counter to what the Bible teaches), a catchy ditty was written for them to sing together at their conferences.

---

[63] Institute in Basic Life Principles, "What is an 'umbrella of protection'?" https://iblp.org/questions/what-umbrella-protection

12 – THE UMBRELLA HERESY—AT HOME AND AT CHURCH

It tells us that when "strong winds blow" and "the cloudburst pours" what will keep these children safe is not God Himself, but being "under the umbrella" over them.

In fact, one line says, *"for protection – that is guaranteed."*[64]

What are they to think except that if they obey their earthly "authority," they will always be physically protected and nothing will ever go wrong for them?

Besides the obvious leaps of illogic noted below, here's another equally obvious but far more significant observation.

These children are not singing about our Lord Jesus Christ and His great salvation, or the greatness of our glorious God.

They're singing about human authorities. This is what would be typical in North Korea . . . or a cult.

What a weird metaphor

As many have noted, an umbrella is an odd choice of metaphors for protection. After all, the truth is that "if strong winds blow," you're not "as safe as you can be"—your umbrella can be ripped to shreds.

And rather than protecting from lightening, an umbrella can actually attract lightening.

> *And also, notice the umbrella handles. The symbolism communicates that none of those "authorities," including God, can shelter anyone unless they're held up. Just imagine trying to hold up multiple umbrellas everywhere you go, every minute of every day, in fear that if you let one slip, some terrible disaster will strike. Some of us don't have to*

---

[64] The Music of the Children's Institute (HQ) "The Umbrella Song" https://www.youtube.com/watch?v=uRdrkzr5IrE.

> *imagine, because we were trying to do it.*[65]

Also, umbrellas offer protection only from rain—and that protection isn't even ideal, since umbrellas work best when the rain is gentle and vertical.

But Gothard needed something *"New."* Something to represent human authority, since there isn't a metaphor for human authority in the Bible.

But instead of protection and provision—which good parents should give to their children even if they don't own any umbrellas—the Umbrella Heresy *applauds control and engenders fear.*

The Umbrella of Control for the Highers

According to Gothard's teachings, which are not found in Scripture, the word of authority must come down from God to the husband/father. This means that the mother, along with the children, *must wait to hear God's word for them from their Umbrella.*

Children, even adult children, and wives (who are adults too!) can't hear from God themselves, can't have independent thought, and can't respond to a calling unless the father/hus-band deems it to be correct.

Controlling men love this. Non-controlling men can become miserable.

> *Whatever God is speaking, he will speak to your husband/father. It doesn't really matter what the topic is: A daughter's future spouse, your callings and responsibilities, how you should spend your time, how you should raise your children. Any decision is between the father/husband and*

---

[65] Comment by Key Truths on "Bill Gothard's Umbrella Heresy in a Day of Protests Against Police Brutality," https://heresthejoy.com/2020/06/bill-gothards-umbrella-heresy-in-a-day-of-protests-against-police-brutality/

12 – THE UMBRELLA HERESY—AT HOME AND AT CHURCH

> *God, and the father/husband will let you know when he is ready to. Your responsibility is to cheerfully go along with it. Even if your father is not a believer . . . you still have to rely on him to be the go-between between you and God.*[66]

The Umbrella of Fear for the Lowers

Fear is the controlling force of the Umbrella Heresy. You stay under the umbrella *because you are afraid.*

> *If you dare to go out from under the umbrella by not conforming perfectly with a joyful countenance and light in your eyes, then any number of hailstorms will pound you to a bloody pulp.*[67]

> *As a teenager, the gradual increase of responsibility would not coincide with a gradual increase in decision-making. A young man would be eligible to step out from under the umbrella of protection only when he married. A young woman would only transfer from the father's umbrella to a husband's. This authoritarian approach forced the fear of both God and parents to become the main reason for obedience.*[68]

The tiny, tiny space of the smallest umbrellas

When I researched this topic, the websites I read were full of testimonies of the crushed children of God who had been pushed down into smaller and smaller spaces, becoming emotionally and spiritually stunted.

---

[66] Dulce Chale, "Peering Underneath the Umbrella: Musings on Gothardism" at https://www.recoveringgrace.org/2012/12/peering-underneath-the-umbrella-musings-on-gothardism/

[67] Ibid.

[68] Derek Lounds, "Growing Up Gothard" at https://www.thegospelcoalition.org/article/growing-up-gothard/

I saw the lives of childhood friends scarred by the umbrella of which you speak. . . . I saw many of them stay well into their thirties, still imprisoned by the umbrella.[69]

There was no graduating to my own umbrella, no trust that I was old enough to think for myself. My parents were still the ones to choose a husband for me. To our peers in the homeschool world, I was considered a child still—even though I was more than 20 years old and held the responsibility of several part-time jobs.[70]

Due to this teaching, I did not develop my own opinions or religious beliefs until years after I left home. The moral decisions that were easy to maintain under my parents' watchful eyes became a challenge to maintain far away from them. At home, I was good at appearing to comply, but my heart wasn't convinced of the truth of some of my parents' convictions. I had no idea how to defend my spiritual beliefs, because I did not "own" those beliefs. Scriptures and principles were simply drilled into my head as trivia to be memorized. Head knowledge does not automatically become heart knowledge.[71]

I totally bought into the umbrella theory in my first (and very abusive) marriage. Sadly, my ex was more like one of those thin plastic camping parkas that stays pretty much in its own little plastic case, and I tended to want to be a large family-sized red and white polka dotted umbrella. He did all

---

[69] Comment from P.L. on "Umbrella of Oppression," at https://www.recoveringgrace.org/2014/05/umbrella-of-oppression/

[70] Michelle, "The Umbrella of Oppression" at https://www.recoveringgrace.org/2014/05/umbrella-of-oppression/

[71] Joy Solano, "The Leaky Umbrella" at https://www.recoveringgrace.org/2011/10/the-leaky-umbrella/

12 – THE UMBRELLA HERESY—AT HOME AND AT CHURCH

he could to squash me and I let him, as a "godly" wife.[72]

The umbrella teaching was what kept me trapped at home until age 29. Because, after all, if I left without parental blessing, I would end up dead in a park like Chandra Levy. It was only after seeing porn frozen all over the home computer that I realized that my "umbrella" had no fabric at all; it was just twisted, broken spokes. That was my epiphany, and two months later, I left that umbrella and reclaimed my life.[73]

Gothard taught the Umbrella hierarchy as within the family, with fathers as the ultimate umbrella.[74]

Under the Umbrella Heresy, adult children can't even access the Lord at all, but have to go through layers of authorities to reach Him. Having one or more Umbrella Persons between God and another adult sets God at a far distance.

But Psalm 145:18 says He has proclaimed Himself to be *near*.

The layers of umbrellas add extra mediators.

But Jesus has said in 1 Timothy 2:5 that *He is the one and only Mediator.*

---

[72] Comment from MeganC on "Spiritual Umbrellas and the Oppression of Women" at https://timfall.com/2017/02/22/spiritual-umbrellas-suppress-women

[73] Comment from Joy T on "Umbrella of Oppression" at https://www.recoveringgrace.org/2014/05/umbrella-of-oppression/

[74] How this is supposed to work when the father is sexually abusing those who are under his protection isn't clear, except that somehow it seems to be implied that their fault if he has holes in his umbrella or his umbrella is completely broken.

It's just so unbiblical

Is rain what we're afraid of?

In the drawing that represents the Umbrella Heresy, Jesus (His "umbrella") covers only a tiny portion of the entire area, and Satan gets all the rest, with his rain.

That is, in all the areas except under your own umbrella hierarchy, Satan is able to reign and rain.

But in reality, *Satan doesn't rain.* Rather, Jesus said,

> "[Y]our Father who is in heaven . . . sends rain on the just and on the unjust." (Matthew 5:45)

When Jesus said that, he was counting rain a blessing, not a punishment or curse. In fact, though rain can be dreary and stormy, Scripture repeatedly refers to it as a good gift sent from God (e.g. Psalm 65:9-13; 147:7-8; Isaiah 55:10-11, Acts 14:16-17).

What metaphors does the Bible really use for Satan's attacks? Not rain, that's for sure. Instead, he walks around like a roaring lion, one that wouldn't be the least bit intimidated by a flimsy umbrella. Or he sends "fiery darts" or "flaming arrows," as Ephesians 6 describes. Umbrellas won't protect you from those—maybe you've noticed that already.

The only thing that will protect you from those is the *shield of faith.* Faith in who? My next-higher-up earthly authority?

No. *Faith in Jesus Christ.*

Having an Umbrella Person as your spiritual protector will keep you in a perpetual state of spiritual childishness and immaturity, when you yourself have been commanded to wear *the full armor of God in Ephesians 6.*

12 – THE UMBRELLA HERESY—AT HOME AND AT CHURCH

A man's authority?

The Umbrella Heresy extends beyond the family, to church leaders, government leaders, and bosses, so that a family cannot leave a cult, Dad cannot leave a job working for an abusive boss, and no one can speak out against government corruption.

This is an equal opportunity heresy. Everybody has to be under some other authority.

Everybody, that is, except, of course . . .

The ultimate Umbrella . . .

Bill Gothard himself.

But for so many years no one questioned this man of God because they believed he delivered the Word of God for his people.

> *The most significant aspect of the teaching on authority was this: Bill Gothard somehow became the ultimate authority over his followers. It was no longer safe to question him or refuse to live by his standards. God and Satan both lurked outside the umbrella, ready to destroy rebellious families.*[75]

But then Gothard was exposed as a scandal-ridden cult leader.[76] His ministry is greatly diminished, and his followers are now few. So surely the Umbrella Heresy can be laid to rest.

Wrong again.

This teaching is alive and well in churches all across the land, even among people who have never heard of Bill Gothard.

And like Gothard, other leaders who hold to this heresy are working to create their own hierarchies, hierarchies in which

---

[75] Sara Jones, "Under the Umbrella," http://www.recovering-grace.org/2015/10/an-ati-education-chapter-1-under-the-umbrella/

[76] Bryan Smith, "The Cult Next Door," *Chicago Magazine*, http://www.chicagomag.com/Chicago-Magazine/July-2016/Institute-in-Basic-Life-Principles-Hinsdale/

they hold ultimate authority and cannot be questioned or challenged.

The Umbrella in the Church

You may have seen the Umbrella Diagram for Reformed churches. That is, this diagram came from some who consider themselves *inheritors of the Reformation,* the revolution when loyalty to the "authority" of the Roman Catholic church was broken and allegiance to the written Word of God and the Living Word of God took preeminence.

In this diagram you'll see Wife and Children at the Bottom, like usual.

The Husband comes next, ostensibly "covering" them.

Then over the husband comes the "Church" or the "Pastor," and then over that is the Umbrella of Christ, with a note under that one that says "Authority to forgive sins passed down to the pastors."

So, Jesus Christ's umbrella "covers" the pastor and passes down to him the authority to forgive sins.

The pastor's umbrella "covers" the husband.

And the husband's umbrella "covers" the wife and children.

The Umbrella Heresy says that one man has the right to pass judgment on the non-sinful decisions and choices of another person, simply because those decisions and choices aren't in line with what the Umbrella Person has said.

But Romans 14:4 says, "Who are you to pass judgment on the servant of another? It is before his own master that he stands or falls. And he will be upheld, for the Lord is able to make him stand."

12 – THE UMBRELLA HERESY—AT HOME AND AT CHURCH

Having an Umbrella Person as your "spiritual covering" means that Jesus Christ Himself is *not sufficient spiritual protection* for you as a Christian. This is heresy.

And yet, just to make sure you understand how ubiquitous this teaching is in Christianity, here are some examples.

The book *You Can Be the Wife of a Happy Husband: Discovering the Keys to Marital Success* describes Christ as being under the umbrella of God the Father (that's heresy right there) and then forming an umbrella for the men of the church, who are then the umbrella for their wives and children.[77]

And it's here in this teaching from Mary Kassian, in an interview with Nancy Leigh DeMoss Wolgemuth of the popular "Revive Our Hearts" radio program:

> . . . [T]he elders of the congregation protect all the women and the men who are under their covering of authority.[78]

Another example makes up the next chapter of this book.

Ultimately this heresy is the recipe for control and fear.

Following Jesus

Where are the Biblical examples of people waiting to get their orders from their earthly authority instead of just following God themselves? David? Jonathan? Daniel? Shadrach, Meshach, and Abednego? Paul? Peter? Stephen? Elijah? Elisha? Esther?

---

[77] Darian Cooper, Destiny Image, 2010. Her description about the umbrella, which sounds exactly like Gothard, is found on pages 91-94, 100-101, 106-109, 137, and 224.

[78] "The Makings of a True Woman." Revive Our Hearts Podcast, June 4, 2008. https://www.reviveourhearts.com/podcast/revive-our-hearts/women-in-the-church-2/

If Martin Luther had followed the Umbrella Heresy, he would never have challenged the Catholic church's false teachings in the Middle Ages. The same goes for all the other Reformers.

The same goes for any Christian who challenges governments that abuse, "law enforcement" officers who are actually criminals, and "church authorities" who use their authority to create cults.

For your spiritual safety, trust not in a man, not in a woman, not in a church, but *in Jesus Christ alone.*

As a commenter on my blog said,

> *This false teaching convinces people that, first and foremost, they need to be fearful of perpetually over-whelming "rain" (calamities, curses, etc.).*
>
> *That the only way to avoid personal eternal disaster is to seek and accept the layers of protection against that rain, of which Jesus is only one layer, and not powerful enough to do the job alone all the way down the line of authority.*
>
> *But biblical truth is the exact opposite. The Lord Jesus Christ is the Light of the World, shining to all people. He is the Sun of Righteousness, with healing in His wings. There is no "rain" that can overcome the sunshine of Jesus.*
>
> *If only I could say to sincere folks caught up in the shady umbrella theology... put down that umbrella and walk in the Light!*
>
> *John 8:12 (NIV) When Jesus spoke again to the people, he said, "I am the light of the world. Whoever follows me will never walk in darkness, but will have the light of life."*[79]

---

[79] Comment by Song of Joy at "An Authority Covering Umbrella of Protection parable, to celebrate the Reformation,"

Though we look to the wise counsel of wise others in our lives, as adults we are responsible for our decisions before our Lord Jesus Christ alone, through His Holy Spirit.

We want to walk in His light.

And when it comes to the spiritual attacks of the enemy, which are numerous, I'll take a shield of faith over an umbrella any day of the week.

An Umbrella Parable

This is a story I posted on my blog in October of 2017, celebrating the 500th birthday of the Reformation.

A monk's experience

Once upon a time, long ago and far away, lived Martin Luther, a fearful and guilt-ridden monk who began actually reading the Bible, which monks were not supposed to do. He received the lightning bolt of revelation of the life of faith in Jesus Christ.

The people over him and the people under him and the people equal to him told him he needed to stay under the covering of his *Umbrella of Protection* that was to be found in his Authority, the Roman Catholic Church (he was a monk, after all).

They said if he stepped out from under this Umbrella, he would be doomed.

But this monk's problem was that he was already doomed, even while he was faithfully under that Umbrella. His heart had never been able to find peace, *until he found it in the Lord Jesus Christ.*

---

https://heresthejoy.com/2017/10/an-authority-covering-umbrella-of-protection-parable-to-celebrate-the-reformation/

As this formerly fearful and formerly guilt-ridden monk drank in the water of the Word of God, he began to see the holes in the Umbrella of Authority and the holes in the *entire paradigm* of the Umbrella of Authority.

He stepped out from under the Umbrella of Authority (the Roman Catholic Church) and out from the entire Paradigm of the Umbrella of Authority. As they persecuted him for doing so, he began to experience the fiery darts of the enemy, which he fought with the shield of faith.

His bold proclamation of the truth, with fearless faith, began what we call the Reformation.[80]

My friend's experience

Once upon a time, not quite so long ago and not quite so far away, a friend showed me her entire correspondence with the pastor of the Reformed church that she eventually left when she escaped her abuser.

All through the first couple of years of that email correspondence, I saw my friend telling her Reformed pastor she wanted to stay under the Umbrella of his Authority and the church's Authority.

I was puzzled as to where she had gotten the term. You see, even though the concept has been around a long, long time, far longer than Martin Luther, the "umbrella" term was a fairly new one. Though I had been one of Bill Gothard's many thousands of

---

[80] When my family and I visited the Bill Gothard Headquarters in Illinois in the early 1990s, I saw two huge portraits on the wall of the office. One was of Gothard's parents. The other was of Martin Luther. Yes, in a supreme irony, Martin Luther—THE person who represents getting out from under human authority!—graced the walls of the headquarters of the Institute in Basic Life Principles.

12 – THE UMBRELLA HERESY—AT HOME AND AT CHURCH

eager listeners, I knew my friend didn't know anything about him.

I asked her where she learned the term.

My friend told me *her Reformed pastor* taught this age-old Umbrella-ism *from his Reformed pulpit,* a lot. He assured his Reformed church members they were "under the Umbrella of Protection of the church." He warned those Reformed church members that if they were to walk away from that Reformed church, they would no longer be under God's protection.

"So." She explained to me what this teaching had communicated to her. "Our salvation was because of the church. And the children's salvation was because of their families who were under the church."

My friend observed that she couldn't remember hearing any preaching about Jesus dying on the cross for us in that Reformed church. Instead, like that fearful and guilt-ridden monk and his peers of old, all eyes were on the church, which meant the pastor.

"The pastor represented God, and we were to huddle under and obey."

My friend eventually got out from under the "Protective Umbrella Covering" of her Reformed church's Authority (which is how I met her).

As she did, the fiery darts she experienced came from that very same so-called "protective covering."

To her relief, as she stayed out from under the "Umbrella of Authority" and drank directly and deeply from the Word of God, she began to experience the rain of God's grace in a way she hadn't in a long time.

This was the beginning of what we might call a new life.

There was once a fearful, guilt-ridden monk—Martin Luther—who became guilt free and bold as a lion when he stepped out from the Paradigm of the Umbrella Heresy.

He is one of the many voices through the generations who has called to us, "Look not to a 'church' for your authority and your spiritual protection. Through the Scriptures alone, and by faith alone, look to Jesus Christ alone."

I ended that 2017 blog post with this:

Happy 500th birthday, Reformation. Together we'll celebrate not only the reign, but the rain, of God's amazing grace.

CHAPTER 13

Your Pastor is Not Moses: a Response to John Bevere's *Under Cover*

A WHILE BACK someone told me that John Bevere's book *Under Cover* had taught "church authority" in such a way that it had nearly destroyed her and her family.

So I bought the book and started reading it.

I saw that the presentation of authority in the book was indeed dangerous, and I might even say *craftily* presented.

First of all, Bevere spends the first 25-30% of the book establishing that God is the ultimate authority. Then throughout the book he keeps coming back to examples of God as the ultimate authority, weaving those examples throughout the rest of the book.

But that's a non-issue for me, because I already believe wholeheartedly in God's authority. I want to follow Him wherever He leads and do whatever He says.

The question comes when talking about any *people* who claim to have spiritual authority. Do they actually have authority over the people of God? If so, what does that look like?

Bevere presents the answer to the first question as an unequivocal and resounding *yes*.

And the answer to the second question is this: You are to be "under the cover" of those who speak from a position of "spiritual authority" in your church. And by the term "spiritual authority," I mean—and he means—"What I'm telling you to do is what God wants you to do."

And by "under cover," of course that means you are to give them unequivocal obedience.

Shades of Umbrellas, perhaps?

In true Gothardesque umbrella-style theology, Bevere says,

> [O]ur judgment will be relative to our submission, for authority is of God. To resist delegated authority is to resist God's authority.[81]

Of course his point all through the book is that God's authority is delegated to the church leader, and as you obey the church leader, you are obeying God.

Here are a few of Bevere's arguments to drive his point home, and my responses.

Bevere compares the man in the position of "church leader" to Moses

Bevere spends several pages (pages 159-163) describing accounts of the failures of the Israelites to follow Moses' divinely-appointed leadership, and what happened to them as a result.

---

[81] John Bevere, *Under Cover: Why Your Response to Leadership Determines Your Future.* Emanate Books, 2018, p. 165.

13 – YOUR PASTOR IS NOT MOSES

He then seamlessly moves into discussion of your pastor. Seamlessly, that is, because he never says, "Your pastor is in the place of Moses." No, what he said is,

> *You may consider yourself wiser than the children of Israel. . . . You would have discerned Moses was right . . . you would have been right there with Joshua.*[82]

See what he did there?

He put you in the place of the Israelites. Then it's a seamless assumption to put your pastor in the position of Moses.

Then he says,

> *What separated Joshua from the rest of his peers was not his discernment, but his ability to recognize and submit to true authority. Out of that came true discernment.*[83]

The implication, of course, is that when and only when you submit to your pastor, you'll be able to discern truth.

Then he moves into the full-blown presentation of your "spiritual leader" as if he is in the place of Moses. But no matter who your pastor is, he doesn't fill the role of Moses.

No, in fact Moses himself said (Deuteronomy 18:15-19),

> *The Lord your God will raise up for you a prophet like me from among you, from your brothers—it is to him you shall listen— just as you desired of the Lord your God at Horeb on the day of the assembly, when you said, "Let me not hear again the voice of the Lord my God or see this great fire any more, lest I die." And the Lord said to me, "They are right in what they have spoken. I will raise up for them a prophet like you from among their brothers. And I will*

---

[82] Ibid., p. 163.
[83] Ibid.

> *put my words in his mouth, and he shall speak to them all that I command him. And whoever will not listen to my words that he shall speak in my name, I myself will require it of him."*

So . . . who was that prophet?

It most certainly was not your pastor.

It was Jesus.

In the days of the Old Covenant, Moses was chosen *directly by God* to lead the Israelites, and that choice was solidified again and again to the Israelites through one miracle after another.

Moses heard directly from God. There were no Scriptures in those days; Moses went up on the mountain and received the words from God. If the Israelites were going to hear anything from God, they had to get it from Moses. He was the intercessor of that day.

But the intercessor of our day is *Jesus*.

We, the New Covenant church, do not need another leader like Moses, because we have *Jesus*. As Hebrews 3:5-6 says,

> *Moses was faithful in God's house as a servant, and he spoke of the things that God would say in the future. But Christ is faithful as the Son in charge of God's house. We are his house if we keep up our courage and our confidence in what we hope for.*

Unequivocally, without a doubt, your pastor does not stand in the place of Moses. He is not delivering the direct word of God. He is not a mediator between God and you.

No, that position has already been filled. Because a greater than Moses is here.

Bevere compares the man in the position of "church leader" to a king

In the same chapter, Bevere uses Esther's approach to the Persian king to show you how you should approach your pastor when you disagree with him.[84]

Obviously when you disagree with someone, you want to be as polite and respectful as possible. But no, Bevere's advice goes way beyond this.

You should approach your pastor as if he is a *king*.

He then backs it up with the story of David's respect toward Saul and Abigail's respect toward David.

You should approach your pastor as if he is a king.

Why does he think there is any parallel between your pastor and a king? What justification does he give? Well, none. He simply smoothly assumes it. Where does this astonishingly heretical teaching come from? Certainly not from the Word of God. Jesus said in Matthew 23:8-12,

> *You must not be called 'Teacher,' because you are all equal and have only one Teacher. And you must not call anyone here on earth 'Father,' because you have only the one Father in heaven. Nor should you be called 'Leader,' because your one and only leader is the Messiah. The greatest one among you must be your servant. Whoever makes himself great will be humbled, and whoever humbles himself will be made great.*

Bevere's teaching, while using Scripture to buttress it, goes completely counter to Scripture.

---

[84] Ibid., pp. 167-168.

Bevere compares the man in the position of "church leader" to the apostle Paul

During our family's church pilgrimage, for a year we were in a denomination that we discovered leaned so far toward pastor worship that it could perhaps have been called cultic. A friend gave me some sermons from the "chief among equals" pastor of a "sister church."

As I listened to him talk about the pastor's authority, I heard him pivot to talk about Paul. I remember thinking, "Oh, he's not going to go there, is he? He's not going to go there?"

But he did. He went there. He said that you are to treat your pastor as the New Testament believers treated the apostle Paul.

I was truly appalled.

There's quite a difference, you know.

Paul was the main one to present God's Word to His New Covenant people. He actually *received the direct word of God.*

If your pastor argues that he also does, well, you could argue the same. Nowhere does the Bible say that a position of church leadership gives a person an inside track to the mind of God.

But not only does Bevere say your pastor is to be honored like the apostle Paul, he takes it a step further, perhaps even further than I've ever heard anyone take this "submission to church authority" thing.

Some back story:

In his first letter to the Corinthians, Paul had told his readers to put a certain man out of the church, a man who was flagrantly living in sin. Then in his second letter to the Corinthians, Paul told them that because the man had repented, they should forgive him, love him, and bring him back into the congregation.

Pretty straightforward.

But here is how Bevere presents it:

> *The apostle Paul told the Corinthian church to do something in his first letter that he altered in his second one. Once he changed his order to the church, he made this remarkable statement: "For this was my purpose in writing you, to test your attitude and see if you would stand the test, whether you are obedient and altogether agreeable [to follow my orders] in everything." (2 Cor. 2:9 AMP).*[85]

Then, contrary to the reality that Paul wanted the Corinthians to follow truth and do the right thing, Bevere says,

> *Paul gave them orders for one purpose: to see whether they would submit to his authority.*[86]

That was a jaw-dropping statement to me. But because Bevere doesn't give any context for Paul's "order reversal," he is able to make it sound completely capricious.

And yes, that's how he follows this up. Keep reading.

> *I have a very wise friend who has been a pastor for years. He told me the way he finds insubordination among his workers is to give a directive that makes no sense. He said, "John, I'll soon hear the gripes and complaints of the rebellious. I deal with it, then change the directive back to normal operations."*[87]

A few sentences later:

> *The purpose: if they followed this directive, they would follow anything else.*[88]

---

[85] Ibid., p. 157.

[86] Ibid., p 175.

[87] Ibid.

[88] Ibid.

Indeed. All the staff members who were actually *thinking*, who realized that to spend time doing a senseless job was a waste of the Lord's time and money, could be kicked out. Only the ones who mindlessly obeyed were kept on.

Is this the way the church of Jesus Christ is supposed to operate?

And no, that wasn't like Paul at all. Not even a little bit.

Besides the fact that Paul's directives in 2 Corinthians did indeed make complete sense, if you'll recall, Paul said in his first letter to the Corinthians (11:1), *"Follow me as I follow Christ."*

And as if that weren't enough . . .

Bevere compares the man in the position of "church leader" to God

Yes, he certainly does.

Bevere tells the story of Moses pleading with the Lord regarding God's decision.

> *First, Moses spoke in complete submission and with fear and trembling. Second, Moses pleaded passionately or petitioned God; he never commanded.*[89]

He then goes on to draw the comparison that you know is coming: this is our guideline for petitioning a church leader.

That is, we are to petition church leaders the same way Moses petitioned God.

Does this seem like idolatry to you?

---

[89] Ibid., p. 173.

Who is your pastor, really?

Your pastor is supposed to be a leader, but not like a general. If we're an army and there's a general, that's Jesus only.

As the next chapter will explain in more detail, your pastor is to be a leader like a guide on an expedition. He is to be one who is farther down the path of life—a little or a lot—and can say, along with others who are elder in the church, "Look! There's Jesus! Let's follow Him!"

That's who your pastor is supposed to be.

But how are pastors often chosen? Well, in many churches, church "pulpit committees" will ask God to help them and will then put out a request for résumés to fill the job.

They'll often look for graduates of certain seminaries, according to their denomination, and perhaps they'll add other qualifiers and administrative strengths, as would an organization looking for a CEO.

After interviews with several prospective leaders, and praying, the committee will then ask one or two of the men to preach. The Sunday the man "candidates" (verb) will often be the first time the church members have met him. There might be a dinner after church so they can talk with him more.

Then the congregation will vote, and if they vote yes, the man is invited to come be the leader of the church.

In another common scenario, a man starts a church on his own, perhaps commissioned by others from somewhere far away. Because something about him is very attractive, usually his speaking ability, and sometimes because he has private investors behind him, he becomes very popular and draws crowds to his church.

The people who flock to the church to hear the popular preacher don't really know what he's like behind closed doors, where he could be living a very different life.

What a far cry from either Moses or Paul this is.

The new pastor that the church members have gone to so much trouble to find, or the man who has started a church "on his own," may be a wolf in sheep's clothing.

After all, it's not that hard for a sociopath to present well for a while, and under certain circumstances.

And wolves love to be in charge of the sheep. That's why "pastor" is one of the most attractive jobs for sociopaths.[90]

These men also love to preach "spiritual authority" the likes of which John Bevere teaches. In fact, I heard from more than one person that *Under Cover* was required reading in their church, and it's no wonder.

That "when I hear from my pastor I'm hearing from God" and "I dare not question my pastor except with fear and trembling like going before a king or God" attitude is exactly what cult leaders love.

True spiritual Christian leaders, on the other hand, will want to faithfully present the Word of God, faithfully walk with those who are on the road of following Jesus, and never consider themselves on a different spiritual plane than the ones they serve.

In a healthy church, the "members," those of us who are "parts of the body," will view the pastor the same way.

John Bevere's *Under Cover* "spiritual authority" sets up a situation that is ideal for a cult to thrive.

This is not what God wants for His people.

---

[90] Lindsay Dodgson, "The 10 professions with the most psychopaths," https://www.businessinsider.com/professions-with-the-most-psychopaths-2018-5

CHAPTER 14

That "Obey Your Leaders and Submit to Their Authority" Scripture: Examining Hebrews 13:17

FOR ANYONE WHO still wants to follow Jesus after having been treated devilishly by those who claim to be His followers (His shepherds, even!), Hebrews 13:17 might stick in the craw.

Here are a few versions you may be familiar with.

> KJV: "Obey them that have the rule over you, and submit yourselves..."

> NIV: "Have confidence in your leaders and submit to their authority..."

> Amplified: "Obey your [spiritual] leaders and submit to them [recognizing their authority over you]..."

And of course that verse is often held over church people's heads, like so:

> *You church people. Unquestioningly obey your "spiritual*

authorities," which is us, the church "leaders." Submit to us without question or challenge. (If you don't, you could be excommunicated and shunned.)

This verse has been used to get church people to check their brains at the door and obey like unthinking robots. (Or if they question, to shame them or formally excommunicate them.)

Can this possibly be true? Can this Scripture really be advocating such cult-like behavior?

To understand, we have to consider several things.

First, there's the context of the whole Bible. It's really amazing how much this is ignored when people choose "proof texts" to wave in other people's faces.

What does God say elsewhere in Scripture about "spiritual authorities"?

This is an important question. Here are a few examples of "spiritual authorities" under the Old Covenant.

> *An appalling and horrible thing has happened in the land: the prophets prophesy falsely, and the priests rule at their direction; my people love to have it so, but what will you do when the end comes?* (Jeremiah 5:30-31)

Do you suppose God would have said to the Israelites, "Obey those spiritual leaders, and submit yourselves?" I think not.

> *And the Lord said to me: "The prophets are prophesying lies in my name. I did not send them, nor did I command them or speak to them. They are prophesying to you a lying vision, worthless divination, and the deceit of their own minds."* (Jeremiah 14:14)

Do you suppose God would have said to those people, "Obey those spiritual leaders, and submit yourselves?" I think not.

> *Thus says the Lord concerning the prophets who lead my people astray, who cry "Peace" when they have something to eat, but declare war against him who puts nothing into their mouths.* (Micah 3:5)

Do you suppose God would have said to those people, "Obey those spiritual leaders, and submit yourselves?" I think not.

And there are the "spiritual authorities" of Ezekiel 34, false shepherds who, instead of caring for the sheep, devoured the sheep.

Do you suppose God would have said to those people, "Obey those spiritual leaders, and submit yourselves?" I think not.

And here are some in the New Testament. Jesus did not mince words about the "spiritual authorities" of His day:

> *Beware of false prophets, who come to you in sheep's clothing but inwardly are ravenous wolves. You will recognize them by their fruits. Are grapes gathered from thornbushes, or figs from thistles?* (Matthew 7:15-16)

In Matthew 23 Jesus cut to shreds these "spiritual authorities," calling them hypocrites, blind guides, whitewashed tombs, full of hypocrisy and lawlessness.

> *You hypocrites! Well did Isaiah prophesy of you, when he said: "This people honors me with their lips, but their heart is far from me; in vain do they worship me, teaching as doctrines the commandments of men."* (Matthew 15:7-9)

Do you suppose He would have told those who wanted to know God to obey those "spiritual authorities" and submit to them? I think not.

So there appear to be plenty of cases where "obey your [supposed] spiritual authorities" doesn't apply.

Both Jesus and Paul warned about false prophets that would lead many astray. Even in the midst of the conservative Reformed, fundamentalist, and other evangelical churches.

> *And many false prophets will arise and lead many astray.* (Matthew 24:11)
>
> *For false christs and false prophets will arise and perform signs and wonders, to lead astray, if possible, the elect.* (Mark 13:22)
>
> *I know that after my departure fierce wolves will come in among you, not sparing the flock; and from among your own selves will arise men speaking twisted things, to draw away the disciples after them.* (Acts 20:29-30)

What should we think about these passages? Should we think that "Obey your spiritual authorities and submit to their authority" applies here?

Well of course, you say, the command doesn't apply to *false* teachers.

But of course those who follow false teachers never think the teachers are false.

That's why it's so easy for the false teachers to secretly bring in destructive heresies.

> *For such men are false apostles, deceitful workmen, disguising themselves as apostles of Christ. And no wonder, for even Satan disguises himself as an angel of light. So it is no surprise if his servants, also, disguise themselves as servants of righteousness.* (2 Corinthians 11:13-15a)

After all, the false teachers, servants of Satan—sometimes directly—do a masterful job disguising themselves as servants of righteousness.

> *For the time is coming when people will not endure sound teaching, but having itching ears they will accumulate for themselves teachers to suit their own passions, and will turn away from listening to the truth and wander off into myths.* (2 Timothy 4:3-4)

I think we can safely say that "obey your leaders and submit to them" doesn't apply to pastors and other leaders who are actually bent on pursuing wickedness.

And in order to recognize such leaders, we have to refrain from turning our brains off and shushing the Holy Spirit when we listen to anyone, including people we have trusted to lead us for a very long time.

> *But false prophets also arose among the people, just as there will be false teachers among you, who will secretly bring in destructive heresies, even denying the Master who bought them, bringing upon themselves swift destruction. And many will follow their sensuality, and because of them the way of truth will be blasphemed.* (2 Peter 2:1-3)

So with all those Scriptures for our framework, let's examine the passage in question, Hebrews 13:17.

Consider each of the 3 key words in the verse

This verse says, "*Obey* your *leaders* and *submit* to them." Obey. Leaders. Submit.

Or in the King James Version, "Obey them that have the rule over you, and submit yourselves."

Yet the Greek word translated "obey" is not the word usually translated "obey" in the New Testament. The Greek word translated "submit" is not the word usually translated "submit." And the Greek word translated "submit" or "have the rule" is not the word usually translated "ruler" or "rule."

So what in the world is Hebrews 13:17 telling us to do?

The word obey

The word most often translated "obey" in the New Testament means "to listen to attentively in order to follow and do what was said." Chapter 8 talks about that word.

This isn't that word.

The meaning of this word is basically "to be persuaded" to change one's beliefs, leading to a change in actions.

Here are a few examples where this Greek word is used of Paul, who was doing the persuading:

- Acts 13:43 Paul *persuaded* the people (to continue in the grace of God)
- Acts 18:4 Paul *persuaded* the Jews and Greeks (to believe in Jesus)
- Acts 19:8 Paul *persuaded* his listeners (about the kingdom of God)
- Acts 19:26 Paul *persuaded* many people (about the Christian way)
- 2 Corinthians 5:11 Paul and friends *persuaded* the people (about the truth of Christianity)

That's the same word as in Hebrews 13:17.

In each case, the people who heard Paul were persuaded to have their thinking changed, which would lead to a change of action. They trusted Jesus Christ and became true Christians.

And a few more examples of people being persuaded, with this same Greek word:

14 – EXAMINING HEBREWS 13:17

- Acts 5:40 the chief priests were *persuaded* by Gamaliel (not to kill the apostles)
- Acts 17:3-4 Some of the people were *persuaded* by Paul's arguments (to believe in Jesus)
- Romans 8:38 Paul was *persuaded* of truth (that nothing could separate him from God's love)
- 2 Timothy 1:5 Paul was *persuaded* of Timothy's faith
- 2 Timothy 1:12 Paul was *persuaded* that Jesus could keep his soul safe
- Hebrews 6:9 The author was *persuaded* that the believers he wrote to were true believers
- Hebrews 11:13 Faithful Hebrews 11 believers were *persuaded* of the promises

As I am *persuaded* to believe what someone has told me, that begins to look like *trust* and *confidence*. So the word is sometimes translated that way too.

Then as my beliefs change, my actions will change accordingly, and that looks like . . . you guessed it . . . *obedience*.

But according to the meaning of this word, that behavioral change that looks like "obedience" is actually supposed to be *a result of thoughtful consideration of a person's sound arguments and evidence*, rather than unthinking robotic compliance.

This is why we can say that Hebrews 13:17 actually says,

"Be persuaded by your leaders."

Now, we all know that there are a few ways to "persuade" someone to change his or her beliefs and then take action accordingly.

1. Sound arguments and real evidence.
2. Upright character.
3. Winsomeness, engaging personality.
4. False arguments and false evidence.
5. "Authority," intimidation, threats, pain, etc.

6. Any combination of 1, 2, and 3.
7. Any combination of 3, 4, and 5.

(Hope that didn't feel like a multiple-choice quiz.)

The Scriptures I cited above were all persuading or being persuaded about something *true*. So they would fit under #1 and #2 above.

But here are some other examples that would fit under #4 (and possibly #3 and #5):

- Acts 14:19 The Jews *persuaded* the people to disbelieve the teachings of Paul.
- Acts 5:36 People were *persuaded* to follow a certain false teacher.
- Acts 5:37 People were *persuaded* to follow another false teacher.

Obviously the persuasion this word points to can be toward something either positive or negative. But there are three uses of this word in the Scriptures in which "authority" definitely plays a part.

- Matthew 27:20 The chief priests used their *authority*—and possibly false arguments, false evidence, intimidation, etc.—to convince the people to choose Barabbas over Jesus.
- Acts 27:11 The centurion decided to obey the *authority* of the ship's pilot (who also owned the ship) to discount Paul's advice, which turned out to be disastrous.
- James 3:3 We use our *authority*—combined with the pain of the bit—to get horses to do our bidding.

Here's the bottom line:

People can be persuaded of something either true or false, in different ways, either good or bad. The same word is used in each case.

We can be confident that God is not saying in Hebrews 13:17 that we should "allow ourselves to be persuaded" by bad church leaders to believe and do something bad.

So it's interesting to find out about that word for "leaders."

"Those who have the rule over you"

I used the King James Version translation there, to give a nod to the huge impact the KJV has had in the life of the Church. (Even though it is no longer the most popular translation, for 400 years it was for all practical purposes the *only* translation.)

Let's just be clear. The KJV "those who have the rule over you" in Hebrews 13:17 is a translation designed to implement church hierarchy along the lines of the Roman Catholics that the translators claimed to disdain. It has been used to buttress significant spiritual abuse through the years.

But interestingly, the Greek word translated "those who have the rule over you" (which in later version was more wisely translated "leader" or "the one leading") also has a verb meaning: *to deem, consider, account, judge, reckon, think, esteem, suppose.* There are about 20 Scriptures using this word with that meaning.

It indicates *making a decision after considering pertinent information and evidence.*

When the word is used of one who leads, then, it means *"one who is considered worthy of leading."*

So . . .

What makes a leader worthy of leading? Any leader at all? Of any kind? In any field?

You consider/deem/judge/account a person worthy of leading you in something because he has been doing this longer than you, he understands it better than you, and he can show you the way.

That means someone who's teaching you how to drive a car or someone who's teaching an online course about scarf acrobatics.

The master chef at the restaurant where you've been hired, or the tech on the other end of the phone who's explaining how to fix your broken website.

You trust the person to know how to do this thing and to be able to explain it to you.

Here is how Steve Smith described it in his pertinent essay on the subject:

> We can picture a guide on a mountainside, leading a group of hikers on a path marked with blazes. The hikers trust the leader because of his demonstrated knowledge and [presumed] good character; and they can see the blazes on the trail as he leads them.[91]

Now, when the "way" being shown involves character and morals at all, there's an added dimension. It's not just about "show me how to do this thing."

It's about—or it certainly should be about—"let me see your life, all of it, so I can know if you're truly living what you teach."

AND when the subject involves Christianity, we have a higher leader than the one at the front of the church building. We have our Lord Jesus Christ, who teaches us through His Scriptures.

We have the Holy Spirit, who helps us—yes, us lowly ordinary Christians—interpret those Scriptures too.

So now we can say, "Let me see your life, all of it, so I can know if you're truly living what you teach and if you're truly living according to the Christian life as described in our higher authority, the Scriptures."

Steve Smith goes on to say about that mountain guide:

---

[91] Stephen Smith, "Hebrews 13:17 in the Greek," August 24, 2012, https://libertyforcaptives.files.wordpress.com/2012/08/hebrews_13_17_in_the_greek.pdf, p 2.

> *However, they do not follow him blindly, as though they wore blindfolds. They would not consent to follow him off a cliff. They are persuaded by his truth and trustworthiness, and they engage critically as they walk along, allowing themselves to be persuaded by him.*[92]

This means keeping the eyes, mind, and heart engaged the entire time. Considering, reckoning, judging.

Luke 22:25-26 and Acts 15:22 are the only Scriptures outside of Hebrews 13:17 that use this same Greek word to refer to "spiritual leaders." Here they are:

> *But [Jesus] said to them, "The kings of the Gentiles lord it over them, and those who exercise authority over them are called 'benefactors.' But it is not this way with you; but let the greatest among you, let him be as the youngest, and he who leads as he who serves."*

> *Then it seemed good to the apostles and the elders, with the whole church, to choose men from among them and send them to Antioch with Paul and Barnabas. They sent Judas called Barsabbas, and Silas, leading men among the brothers.*

The one who leads is to be as the one who serves.

Judas Barsabbas and Silas had shown themselves to be worthy leaders. Was it by bossing others around and demanding unquestioning obedience? No, I believe it's appropriate to assume that *they showed themselves to be worthy leaders by doing what Jesus had said, serving.*

---

[92] Ibid. In regard to this: "They would not consent to follow him off a cliff," I've heard more than one Brother So and So say if their pastor told them to jump off a cliff, they would do it. And they're proud of their blind obedience and sheer idiocy.

In his helpful article on Hebrews 13:17, Ron from scripturerevealed.com said

> *Hebrews 13:17 is clearly not a license for men to dictate, rule, control, command, dominate, and otherwise exercise authority over others in the church. We know this first and foremost because Jesus and His Apostles told us that such things are forbidden!*[93]

Where did Jesus say "such things are forbidden"?

> *But Jesus called them and said, You know that the rulers of the nations exercise dominion over them, and they who are great exercise authority over them. However, it shall not be so among you. But whoever desires to be great among you, let him be your servant. And whoever desires to be chief among you, let him be your servant; even as the Son of Man did not come to be served, but to serve, and to give His life a ransom for many. (Matthew 20:25-28)*

And Peter talked about it too.

> *I exhort the elders who are among you, I being also an elder and a witness of the sufferings of Christ, and also a partaker of the glory that shall be revealed. Feed the flock of God among you, taking the oversight, not by compulsion, but willingly; nor for base gain, but readily; nor as lording it over those allotted to you by God, but becoming examples to the flock. (1 Peter 5:1-3)*

Rather than pulling rank and lording it over others, a true shepherd will be compassionate and loving. He won't intimidate, shame, or blame the sheep.

Many years ago, I wrote to a friend:

---

[93] Ron, "The Hebrews 13:17 Dilemma," at https://www.scripturerevealed.com/the-church/the-hebrews-1317-dilemma/

14 – EXAMINING HEBREWS 13:17

A quotation I read bothered me a little. It said, "God uses people in three ways: to reveal our sin, to help us to take action against our sin, and to walk with us in our struggle against sin."

It bothered me because I want to think that my primary help to my brothers and sisters is not about sin. It's about the Savior. It's saying, "Look, friend! There's Jesus! Let's follow Him together!"

I said it again as part of a blog post:

I want the record of my life to be that I have been found faithful. I want to continue to have increasing understanding of the truths that our God has proclaimed in His Word and in His world, and proclaim those beautiful truths to others. I want to continue learning and seeking and knowing the true Lord Jesus Christ, in all His power and glory, and point others to Him. "Look—there's Jesus! Let's follow Him together."[94]

When I studied this passage of Scripture, I saw that what I've thought a Christian leader ought to be—someone farther down the path of the Christian life (a little or a lot), pointing the way to Jesus—is just what Hebrews 13:17 is referring to.

A worthy church leader will give evidence of a life worth following. So consider, reckon, watch for the fruit. And remember: Public evidence, by itself, can be deceiving. The kind of public evidence that some find most alluring may also be the most misleading: charisma, speaking ability, fund raising ability, marketing ability, photo ops, books written, impressive connections, public relations, and a full calendar on the conference circuit.

---

[94] "What if Your Life Were Written as a Story," at https://www.heresthejoy.com/2019/09/reflections-on-my-62nd-birthday-what-if-your-life-were-written-as-a-story/

Simply put, a life worth following is a life of integrity, in regard to love for Jesus, with the leader being the same person in public, in private (with a few select people the leader trusts) and in secret (when the leader is alone).

Do you think God could in any universe want His people to follow church leaders who fail to live wholehearted lives of integrity?

When we see what the first two key words in this verse really tell us, we can be confident that THIS is what the author of Hebrews meant when he wrote about the "leaders" of the Christian churches:

Be persuaded by (or "let yourself be persuaded by") the ones who have been recognized as being farther along in their lives of faith than you are, who have shown by their wholehearted integrity that they can point the way to Jesus.

And finally, the last key word from this Scripture.

"Submit to them"

There is a Greek word translated *submit* that means "listen to instructions and follow through."

This word doesn't mean that. This is a different word.

There's something tricky about it, though. Hebrews 13:17 is the only place this word is used in the entire Bible. So the idea of submission needs to be held in light of the previous two words.

Again, Ron at scripturerevealed.com says:

> *Since it is already qualified by the requirement to "be persuaded" before you "submit," this verse cannot be used to advocate blind obedience that is sometimes required by leaders. We are required to "submit" to those things that we can "be persuaded" are true according to the Word of God.*
>
> *There is a dangerous false teaching that says that even if we*

do not agree with church leaders we are to "submit" and somehow we will be blessed. This teaching is not backed up by the scriptures.

The obedience and submission required by Hebrews 13:17 is about instruction in the Word of God. It is about having the heart of a humble servant. It is about following a religious leader who is proclaiming truth and holiness.

The submission required by Hebrews 13:17 is not an absolute submission without qualification. It is submission based on the will of God as revealed in His Word. Every Christian is responsible for studying to show themselves approved and to rightly divide the Word of truth.[95]

Seek the "godly" ones

Not those with the appearance of godliness

There's one more Scripture I want to mention, 2 Timothy 3:1-5. It tells us that there are some who "have the appearance of godliness"—hmm, wonder what that looks like—who are actually lovers of self and money and pleasure, proud and arrogant, abusive, and more.

But they "appear" to be godly.

If they are leaders, should we obey and submit to them, according to Hebrews 13:17?

Some will say—I hear it now—*my* pastor will show me how to recognize these false prophets. I have faith in him.

And yet I've also heard that some of those "pastors" who are most eager to preach against "what to watch out for," are doing

---

[95] Ron, "The Hebrews 13:17 Dilemma," at https://www.scripturerevealed.com/the-church/the-hebrews-1317-dilemma/

evil themselves in secret. I know this because former wives and adult children of pastors have spoken to me.

You need to be following Jesus yourself

You know it's a problem to let one man, or even a group, interpret the Bible for you. As one commenter on my blog said,

> *It became easy with the onslaught on these rogue teachers to become deceived into things. Instead of reading scripture, allowing the Holy Spirit to speak to us, we allowed other deceptive teaching in our lives to lead us astray. We took their word for it. We let others be our watchman. We took their interpretation of scripture and put it above the Bible.*[96]

Paul said that the very purpose of having spiritual leaders is

> *So that we may no longer be children, tossed to and fro by the waves and carried about by every wind of doctrine, by human cunning, by craftiness in deceitful schemes. Rather, speaking the truth in love, we are to grow up in every way into him who is the head, into Christ. (Ephesians 4:14-15)*

After all, you're supposed to be following the Word of God on your own. If you're a believer in Jesus, you also have the Holy Spirit and also can be listening to His voice. And if we allow others to interpret the Bible for us, aren't we simply falling into the way of the Middle Ages Catholics—the very problem that the Reformation came to . . . reform?

> *Do not be led away by diverse and strange teachings, for it is good for the heart to be strengthened by grace. (Hebrews*

---

[96] Comment by Bunkababy on "'Biblical' patriarchy: here's how you replaced God" at https://heresthejoy.com/2017/07/christian-patriarchy-heres-how-you-have-left-god/

13:9)

Can it really be, in contradiction to ALL those verses above, that Hebrews 13:17 will now tell us to turn off our brains and slavishly obey our "spiritual authorities"?

> *Beloved, do not believe every spirit, but test the spirits to see whether they are from God, for many false prophets have gone out into the world.* (1 John 4:1)

No. According to many other Scriptures, you should never, never check your brain and spirit at the door and simply comply without questioning. Always you should be listening critically and asking the Holy Spirit for confirmation and discernment, whether what you're hearing is true.

> *Finally, be strong in the Lord and in his mighty power. Put on the full armor of God, so that you can take your stand against the devil's schemes. For our struggle is not against flesh and blood, but against the rulers, against the authorities, against the powers of this dark world and against the spiritual forces of evil in the heavenly realms. Therefore put on the full armor of God, so that when the day of evil comes, you may be able to stand your ground, and after you have done everything, to stand.* (Ephesians 6:10-13)

You have a responsibility.

The ideal leader-follower relationship

From Steve Smith at libertyforcaptives.com.

> *Hebrews 13:17 does not imply blind obedience to spiritual authorities, nor should it ever be invoked by a spiritual leader in order to coerce or compel people to obey them.*

> *Instead, it is a reminder that spiritual leaders in the church who are trustworthy and who proclaim the truth are in a place of persuasive guidance that fellow believers should yield to. If leaders demonstrate these criteria, we should allow ourselves to be persuaded by them for our own good on the rocky path of life.*[97]

What a delight this will be, when we Christians, all of us, leaders official and unofficial, can turn to those of us a bit behind us on the path of the Christian life and say to each other, "Look! There's Jesus, the Good, Holy, and True God. Let's follow Him together!"

Even in a life of sorrow and pain, this can be a Christian experience of joy.

---

[97] Steve Smith, "Hebrews 13:17: Spiritual Authority's Most Abused Verse," at https://libertyforcaptives.com/2012/08/24/hebrews-1317-spiritual-authoritys-most-abused-verse/

CHAPTER 15

"Loyalty" is Not a Christian Virtue

WHEN I WAS a young graduate assistant working at Bob Jones University (learning publishing at BJU Press), like all the other employees I was given certain odious assignments to fulfill each semester, such as monitoring the "dating parlor" for a couple of hours on a Sunday.

One Sunday after I had finished that assignment, my replacement came along, a BJU lifer, Miss Potts. She asked me if I was going to obediently head on over to Vespers (the University's drama program presented on Sunday afternoons).

"No," I responded somewhat defiantly. "I'm going to church."

Miss Potts was an old Southern lady with an absolutely perfect Southern drawl. "The Univuhsity," she said, "would want you to go to Vespuhs."

And there a loyal generation and a . . . different generation went head to head with the loyalty issue.

What does the entity-without-a-face, "the Univuhsity," want me to do?

"Well," I said, hoisting my bookbag to my shoulder, "I think the Lord would want me to go to church."

And I left before she could respond again.

Now my point here isn't whether or not going to church was the absolute best thing I could have done with my time at that moment. (As far as I know now, it still was.)

It's a question of *loyalty*.

What in the world is it, why is it so touted in Christian circles, and why am I saying it's not Christian?

It came up in a phone conversation with someone recently when she was accused by others of "disloyalty." I said, "Yes, I wrote a blog post about that many years ago."

It came up again not so long ago when I read Deborah Brunt's exposé of the Southern Baptist convention on her blog, Key Truths, gently written yet exposing brutal truths.[98]

Have you ever, when reading the negative things someone says about an institution to which they devoted many years of their lives—say, me, when I learned and grew so much at BJU-Press and have such great appreciation for those who taught me there—have you ever wondered why they *would be so disloyal* as to call out problems or perceived problems in that very institution?

Like, say, the way I and some friends did for several years on BJUGrace[99]? The way Deborah Brunt has done about the SBC[100]? The way many other Jesus-followers have done about their former churches and other institutions?

Seems like it's time to examine loyalty.

---

[98] Deborah Brunt, "Behind the Façade in the SBC," https://www.key-truths.com/behind-the-facade-in-the-sbc/

[99] www.bjugrace.com

[100] https://www.keytruths.com/?s=Baptist

What is loyalty?

The fact is that the concept of loyalty fits more with the feudal system than with Christianity.

It was first used of knights swearing allegiance to kings, to fight for that king and no other king. It indicated an *underling* and an *overlord*, as well as a strong sense of "My king, right or wrong." Because *loyalty is unswerving.*

However . . .

This concept of loyalty isn't in the Bible. It just isn't. No place.

What God's Word teaches is *faithfulness: always in love seeking the other's good.* People often use the word *loyal* to describe what husband and wife should be to each other, but *faithful* is a far better word.

This examination of terminology sheds a whole new light on the issue.

Loyalty implies sticking with the organization without asking questions.

Faithfulness demands reciprocal questions when necessary.

Loyalty will go to bat for the institution without understanding the issues.

Faithfulness will do the hard thing to actually look at what's going on, even if the answer gives a gut punch.

Loyalty says, "I will simply assume that this organization is faithful to God."

Faithfulness says, "I'll drag these issues [sometimes issues no one else is talking about yet but which are in the warp and woof of the organization] out into the light and examine them in the light of God's Word."

Because faithfulness *puts God and God's truth and God's love first.*

Faithfulness over loyalty

True faithfulness is willing to question authority. True faithfulness won't turn a blind eye and a deaf ear to those who say, "There is a problem."

True faithfulness knows that when those who work in an institution are promoting to the public a presence of peace and joy but behind the scenes are living in fear of the senior pastor, *there is a huge problem that needs to be addressed.*

Even though you, a lover of Jesus Christ, you would never say, *"My church/ university/ denomination/ mission board, right or wrong,"*

. . . even though you would never say that . . .

if you stand by the concept of institutional loyalty, *this may well be how your loyalty ultimately plays out in your life.*

You may end up putting someone or something else in place of God in your life.

And isn't this one of the things you've warned others against?

Where will you stand?

Will you be faithful to God and His Word as we look at the possibility that an organization may be systemically corrupt (because the leaders and possibly even the founders are/were corrupt)? Will that shake you to the core too deeply? How big is your God?

Will you look the other way because you've committed yourself never to speak evil of your leaders, the way the loyal knight never questioned his regent?

Will you refuse to listen to or speak about any of the wrongs you see or hear about lest you be gossiping?[101]

In the name of "serving the church,"[102] will you offer blind loyalty to leaders who need to be questioned?

In the name of "erring on the side of grace,"[103] will you refuse to listen to evidence against a hero of yours?

Will you turn away from this talk, labeling it "negative"[104]?

Will you determine that you will never say anything that could harm a leader's reputation[105]? *There are so, so many reasons to be loyal.*

All of them carefully crafted, carefully put in place, by those who want to retain your loyalty. Unquestioning.

Because if you question, of course, it's not really loyalty, now, is it?

True faithfulness implies mutuality among the followers of God

As Hebrews 3:13 says, we *"Exhort one another daily, while it is called today, lest any be hardened through the deceitfulness of sin."*

---

[101] https://heresthejoy.com/2019/04/those-renegade-bloggers-in-the-christian-post/

[102] https://heresthejoy.com/2016/11/what-does-it-mean-to-serve-the-church/

[103] https://heresthejoy.com/2017/11/erring-on-the-side-of-grace-when-it-comes-to-repentance/

[104] https://heresthejoy.com/2018/09/why-are-you-so-negative-a-response-to-positive-people/

[105] https://heresthejoy.com/2018/10/is-exposing-evildoers-a-violation-of-the-ninth-commandment-a-response-to-tim-challies-part-one/

It was *faithfulness* that the prophet Nathan showed to King David when he confronted him, rather than "loyally" keeping his mouth shut about David's sin.

If one person is doing wrong as clearly delineated in the Bible (rather than as determined by extra-Biblical standards), another who loves God and loves others would be *faithful* to come alongside and say, *"You're on the wrong path. Here's the right path. Turn and go that way. Turn now."*

This isn't "loyalty." But this is faithfulness. A faithfulness that embodies *mutuality, maturity, responsibility,* and *integrity,* virtues in which all of us should be growing.

Are you faithful?

Will you be faithful to follow Jesus Christ, even if it means losing nearly everything? This is what happened to Deborah Brunt in the Southern Baptist Convention.[106] It has happened to many others I know as well.

They are faithful to Jesus Christ, following Him still, even when they have lost nearly everything because of the entity-with-many-faces institutions that they were told they had to follow, in order to follow Him.

It could be that some Christian institutions need to be dissolved because they are completely corrupt at the highest and deepest levels.

But I, along with many others, do still hope for better things ahead.

And we ask God for the grace and perseverance to faithfully continue on. With loyalty to none. And, in Christ, faithfulness to all.

---

[106] https://www.keytruths.com/this-girl-is-a-woman-now/

PART FOUR

The Authority of Jesus . . . and Us

CHAPTER 16

Jesus vs. the Pharisees

WHEN YOU ACTUALLY look at the Scriptures and see how Jesus reacted to the "spiritual leaders" of His day, the scribes, Pharisees, and teachers of the law—one thing you might notice is that He wasn't excited about telling the people to obey them.

Yes, it's true that in Matthew 23:2-3a Jesus said, "The scribes and the Pharisees sit on Moses' seat [teaching the Word of God], so do and observe whatever they tell you. . . ."

This may sound like no matter how evil the lives of leaders might be (the Pharisees were very wicked), it doesn't matter. Still, you should obey what they tell you.

But when we take this with other Scriptures, we get a different picture.

In Matthew 16:6, Jesus said to his disciples, "Watch and beware of the leaven of the Pharisees and Sadducees." Verse 12 explains that "leaven" refers to the *teaching* of the Pharisees and Sadducees.

Do and observe what they tell you when they teach the true Word of God. But watch out for teachings that are added to the Word of God.

In the rest of Matthew 23, Jesus blasted the scribes and Pharisees for their utter hypocrisy.

The hypocrites

When the Pharisees are portrayed or described today, we think about them as obviously pompous, obviously arrogant, and obviously hypocritical.

But to the Jewish people, their hypocrisy wasn't obvious at all.

You may think that this is because they were naïve, and you wouldn't have been so naïve? Well, maybe not. But perhaps there are some among us today who have been deceived by church leaders who, to our shock, we have found to be hypocrites, leaders who claimed to be building the Kingdom of the Savior, and we find out that all along they were building a kingdom for themselves.

Yes, I raise my hand. I've been deceived by leaders that I thought truly followed Jesus Christ, who turned out to be hypocrites like the Pharisees, or worse.

That's how good they are at the games they play.

And the religious leaders in Jesus' world were just that good.

This is why the crowds were shocked—*shocked*—when during His 3½ years of public ministry, Jesus called out the religious leaders as vipers, whited sepulchers, and more.

In those days, the Jews had two sets of "governments." The Roman overlords were the hated foreigners (picture Nazi Germany having conquered the United States, and American street corners swarming with German soldiers).

But as much as the Jews hated the Romans, the Roman government stayed out of Jewish religious affairs. If the Jews had wanted to hold a lynching because someone claimed to be a messiah figure, the Romans would have looked the other way, as long as the mob didn't get too unruly.

Basically, as long as the Jews obeyed Roman law, the Romans just didn't care what they believed or practiced.

16 – JESUS VS. THE PHARISEES

And that leads us to that other government. The religious "authorities."

When Jesus was arrested and brought to the Roman governor Pilate, the Roman soldiers did indeed take advantage of the opportunity to mock and torture a man who couldn't defend himself: they were the ones who applied the crown of thorns and the purple robe, spitting in His face and slapping and beating Him.

But those opportunistic bullies had no idea who He was. After all, they didn't care one way or another about a solitary man who wasn't stirring up any trouble.

The ones who knew who Jesus was? They were the ones who came for him in the Garden of Gethsemane in the middle of the night. They were the lackeys of the religious leaders, and perhaps even some of the religious leaders themselves.

And the first physical persecution of Jesus? At that very first secret trial in the middle of the night, that wasn't Roman soldiers. No, Mark 14:65 and Luke 22:63-65 tell us that it was the "godly" religious leaders who spat on Him and struck Him and mocked Him.

That is the depths to which they sank.

And my guess is, they would go out the next day and gently instruct their disciples in the finer points of what it means to honor God with their lives.

Because the best hypocrites are amazing like that.

And oh, did I say secret trial? When I was reading about it, my mind flashed to a secret trial held over a friend of mine, a group of men against her, proclaiming her judgment, because she had reported her abusive husband. But they are highly respected religious leaders, with many truly adoring followers who refuse to hear anything against their leaders.

You may know of other secret meetings at which those who are highly respected have done terrible things to innocent ones. These abused ones have shared in the sufferings of Jesus.

Jesus knows

Those highly respected leaders in the Bible (respected by followers who were no more naïve than many of us have been) are the ones who decided that Jesus should die because He was usurping their place, attracting their followers to Himself.

And they decided that they wanted Him to die in the most excruciating and ignominious way possible, *simply because they hated Him that much.*

That's why they didn't arrange for thugs to kill Him in the night. That's why they aroused the crowd so that they could get Pilate to hang a man on a Roman cross—*a man he knew was innocent.*

To see the depths of darkness these religious leaders were in, were *already* in: When Judas came back to tell them Jesus was innocent (Matthew 27), their reply, basically, was, "Why are you talking about that? That's not our problem. That's your problem."

You think we care about guilt and innocence? Oh hahaha.

You've suddenly developed a conscience? That just gets in the way around here.

Oh, he's returning the money we gave him to betray his friend to death? Well, it's "blood money," you know, so we probably shouldn't put that in the temple fund, but we can use it to buy that sweet piece of property over there.

We will "keep the law" (mint, rue, anise, micro-doctrine that we elevate to the level of salvation), but we will proudly (behind the scenes, of course, in secret and in the cover of darkness) thumb our noses at justice, mercy, and truth.

Truly this is why Jesus said during the arrest (in Luke 22:53), "But this is your hour, *and the power of darkness.*"

It was the power of darkness—devilish, satanic power—fueling these men, for all their humble looks and earnest sermons and gentle admonitions and quiet (but spoken) prayers in the streets.

Jesus knew, all along. He knew exactly how it was all going to shake out. He knew that the visceral, demonic hatred of the "godly" religious leaders would lead to His death.

He knew that, even when He called them out, publicly, in the streets of Jerusalem, in Matthew 23:13.

"Woe to you, scribes and Pharisees, hypocrites!"

He knew.

And He moved forward anyway, doing what His Father had called Him to do, facing the horror and staring it down.

He is our wonderful, beautiful, strong, and loving Example and Savior. In spite of any religious leaders who try to block the way, we will run to Him.

After all, He wins in the end.

CHAPTER 17

Thoughts for the Hopeless from Isaiah 40

SO WHAT'S THE truth about authority?

When it comes to adults, does anyone have any "Boss-type" spiritual authority?

Well, God does, that's for sure. And as God in the flesh, our Lord Jesus Christ does.

Let's press into that in what might be a somewhat unexpected way.

Isaiah chapter 40 shows the God of heaven to be truly the ultimate Authority, exalted and glorious. From verse 12 to the end of the chapter in verse 31, God is shown to be high and lifted up.

Here are verses 12-17, using metaphors to help us get the barest glimpse of the high exalted authority of our great God.

> *Who has measured the waters in the hollow of his hand*
> *and marked off the heavens with a span,*
> *enclosed the dust of the earth in a measure*
> *and weighed the mountains in scales*
> *and the hills in a balance?*
> *Who has measured the Spirit of the Lord,*
> *or what man shows him his counsel?*

> *Whom did he consult,*
>   *and who made him understand?*
> *Who taught him the path of justice,*
>   *and taught him knowledge,*
>   *and showed him the way of understanding?*
> *Behold, the nations are like a drop from a bucket,*
>   *and are accounted as the dust on the scales;*
>   *behold, he takes up the coastlands like fine dust.*
> *Lebanon would not suffice for fuel,*
>   *nor are its beasts enough for a burnt offering.*
> *All the nations are as nothing before him,*
>   *they are accounted by him as less than nothing and emptiness.*

But when I was pondering and meditating over this Scripture one day, my eyes came back to verses 10 and 11. Verse 10 begins,

> *Behold, the Lord God (Adonai Jehovah) comes with power, and His arm rules for Him.*

That sounds intimidating, and appropriately so, because we're talking about the God of heaven and Lord over the whole earth, glorious and mighty.

His reward

> *Behold! His reward is with Him, and His recompense is before Him.*

That's interesting. So what is His reward and His recompense? What reward and recompense will be great enough for a God that holds the waters of the earth in the hollow of His hand and measures the dust of the earth in His scales, who counts the nations as a drop in a bucket and brings the princes of the earth to nothing (as the rest of the chapter describes)?

What reward could this infinitely glorious God be referring to?

17 – THOUGHTS FOR THE HOPELESS FROM ISAIAH 40

How arresting it is then, to see this next verse, verse 11. It seems almost out of place, describing His reward and His recompense. Read it closely:

> *He will tend his flock like a shepherd; he will gather the lambs in his arms; he will carry them in his bosom, and gently lead those that are with young.*

Do you see? Do you see there what his reward is?

His reward is with Him, and they are His reward.

The Hebrew word translated "recompense" (basically the same thing as "reward") can also be rendered "work" or "labor."

> *Behold! His reward is with Him, and His work is before Him.*

If we read verse 10 that way, and then come to verse 11, we can immediately see what His work is.

Tending His flock.

Gathering the lambs in His arms.

Carrying them in His bosom.

Gently leading the ewes who are heavy with young.

This is the introduction to the God who is described in the rest of the chapter as so awesome there is absolutely no one and nothing on this earth that can compare with Him.

The same arm that rules in power is the arm that tenderly gathers up the lambs and carries them.

This is our God. The one who is gloriously exalted, the one who comes with ruling power.

He is also the one who would never hurt His own sheep. Instead, He delights to do the tender work of leading, gathering, carrying, and caring.

But there's another thing to notice.

Lift up your voice

It's the verse just before this, verse 9. In it, the mountains of Zion and of Jerusalem are called on to shout out the good news with a loud voice.

> *Go on up to a high mountain,*
>   *O Zion, herald of good news;*
> *lift up your voice with strength,*
>   *O Jerusalem, herald of good news;*
>   *lift it up, fear not;*
> *say to the cities of Judah,*
>   *"Behold your God!"*

"Lift up your voice!" says the prophet. "Don't be afraid! Go up on a mountain and shout it to all the cities of Judah. 'Look! Here is your God!'"

So here I am. Picture me on a mountaintop, along with many others.

Look! Here is your God. We're telling you, unafraid, shouting it from the mountaintop. *Here is your God!*

It is Jesus Christ, the Lord God of heaven and earth, who comes with power and might against the wicked, but who died on the cross and rose again to gain His reward.

And that reward He tenderly gathers and cares for: His own sheep who compose His flock and who follow Him, putting their faith and trust in Him.

Did I hear you say, "No, this is for others, it's not for me. It's not for me"?

I'm telling you, if you have trusted in Jesus Christ to save you— no matter how small and weak your faith may be—this is for you.

It's for you if you're struggling with hoping that God is good, or that He loves you. It's for you if you're filled with fear because in His awesome authority (and it is awesome!) you fear He may destroy you . . .

Please remember this picture in Isaiah 40: the mighty Shepherd tenderly carrying the lambs in His arms. Please know that if you put your faith in Jesus Christ, He will love you, comfort you, and be with you, even in the darkest night.

You are His reward.

More in chapter 62

In chapter 62 Isaiah speaks some similar words, with a slight enlargement of meaning. Verse 11 echoes words from chapter 40:

> *Behold, the LORD has proclaimed to the end of the earth: Say to the daughter of Zion, "Behold, your salvation comes! Behold, his reward is with him, and his recompense [or work] is before him."*

In chapter 40, the reward was His flock. How is it described here? Verse 12 tells:

> *And they shall be called "The Holy People," "The Redeemed of the LORD"; and you shall be called "Sought Out, A City Not Forsaken."*

This is His reward.

You who have trusted in Jesus Christ, don't lose sight of hope. In all of His mighty, powerful, awesome authority, He treasures you. He rejoices over you. You are holy and redeemed. You are sought out and not forsaken. You are tenderly loved.

The Father, this Father, this God of all creation, with all authority over the whole universe . . .

This God . . . loves you. You are His delight.

You are His reward.

You can carry with you words of hope from our Lord Jesus Christ, found in Luke 12:32.

> *"Fear not, little flock, for it is the Father's good pleasure to give you the Kingdom."*

This is good news. This is great joy.

CHAPTER 18

The Authority We Have in Jesus Christ

THE SUBJECT OF our authority in Jesus Christ is a big one. Entire books have been written about it. But in a book that addresses false authority, I feel compelled to at least give a brief introduction to the true authority the Lord Jesus has given those who trust in Him.

This flows out of the teaching in the previous chapter.

Before Jesus left this earth in victory to be seated at the right hand of the Father, He said some important words to His disciples in Matthew 28:18.

> *"All authority in heaven and on earth has been given to me."*

Ten days later, His followers, received the Holy Spirit, who is the Spirit of Christ.

Where is our authority?

We who trust in the Lord Jesus Christ serve under Him, who has *all* authority. And He has delegated certain authority to each of us who trust in Him. But it's not over other people.

In this world, there is a realm of the seen (the physical realm) and the realm of the unseen (the spiritual realm). Ephesians 2:6 tells us that God the Father

> *Raised us up with him [Jesus] and seated us with him in the heavenly places in Christ Jesus.*

This seating of authority has already happened, but it can't mean we're in heaven now (because we're not). The authority we have is in the spirit realm, over spiritual entities. That is, because we are in Jesus Christ, we have authority over evil spirits.

This authority we have is not about asking God for something. Asking is a legitimate aspect of true prayer, but that's not what we're talking about here.

This authority is about *declaring* something, or making a *command*. That's what authority is. And not declaring or commanding in this physical realm for our own benefit. But declaring and commanding in the spiritual realm for the Kingdom of God.

While acknowledging the sin we all fall prey to, the power of "the world" and "the flesh," I want to focus here on the work of "the devil." As representatives of the Lord Jesus Christ, his realm is one over which we have authority.

I have a theory. This theory is born out of years of listening to abuse survivors' stories.

Those cultic religious leaders I've been talking about in the rest of the book? I believe that keeping us confused and under their thumb is one way *Satan keeps us from recognizing our true authority.*

The devil fears Christians who understand their identity in Jesus Christ and their true place in the Kingdom of God and the authority we thus have in Jesus Christ, in the spirit realm.

Satan does not want us to know who we really are.

18 – THE AUTHORITY WE HAVE IN JESUS CHRIST

What Jesus has given

In the previous chapter I noted that Jesus said in Luke 12:32,

> *"Fear not, little flock, for it is the Father's good pleasure to give you the Kingdom."*

We are heirs of the Kingdom, heirs of the *Kingdom of our Lord Jesus Christ.*

As heirs, every one of us who trusts in Jesus Christ has authority in Him over the forces of evil.

All of us, from the "lowest" to the "highest." All those who trust in Jesus. He has delegated authority to us to command the enemy out and away, in the Name and by the authority of the true Lord Jesus Christ, the only begotten Son of God.

For me, it was a long time before I personally learned this in my experience. When the Holy Spirit led me to listen to the painful stories of those who have been abused and oppressed by religious leaders, that's when I became aware of evil on a greater scale. This led to the opening of my eyes to the constant warfare going on in the spirit realm, as demonic forces battle against the Kingdom of God.

As I've continued in this work, I've realized at a deeper and deeper level that there is much spiritual warfare to be done.

After all, a primary way the devil accomplishes his evil work is when humans believe his lies and act on them.

If you are a child of God, the devil knows you have great authority. And he doesn't want you to know it.

Do you know it?

My book *Prayer Armor for Defense against the Enemy's Flaming Darts*[107] goes more deeply into this concept of spiritual

---

[107] Pennycress Publishing, 2019.

warfare and the authority we have over the enemy in our personal lives. But what a shame that many churches—especially many coming from a more fundamentalist, Reformed, or conservative evangelical perspective—don't teach this authority at all.

Yes, there are some churches, some who call themselves Christians, who go to extremes with seeing the devil and his minions everywhere. Yes, there are some who even use this truth about spiritual authority as one more way to abuse innocent people.

But as we humbly examine the Word of God and listen to His Holy Spirit, we will be able to embrace what God has said is true. Many passages in the New Testament refer to spiritual warfare. Ephesians 6:10-13 is perhaps the best known one.

> *Finally, be strong in the Lord and in the strength of his might. Put on the whole armor of God, that you may be able to stand against the schemes of the devil. For we do not wrestle against flesh and blood, but against the rulers, against the authorities, against the cosmic powers over this present darkness, against the spiritual forces of evil in the heavenly places. Therefore take up the whole armor of God, that you may be able to withstand in the evil day, and having done all, to stand firm.*

Defensive and offensive

In *Prayer Armor for Defense against the Enemy's Flaming Darts*, I walk the reader through a *defensive* prayer, with its Scriptural foundation. That is, a prayer of authority against the enemy to protect us from his attacks in the life of our thoughts and emotions.

But Christians can engage in warfare *offensively* as well, to help rescue souls who are under the enemy's control. You might even say this is when our authority can become more obvious.

Who is affected by evil spirits?

Though many Christians would like to live as if there is no battle going on in the unseen realm and there are no evil spirits and there is no work of the devil (only "the world" and "the flesh"), the battle is real.

I believe the New Testament clearly shows two types of people in Jesus' time who were demonized, that is, afflicted by demons. (I use the term "demonized" rather than "demon possessed" because it is more accurate to the original Greek and it allows for different degrees or types of demonic activity in a person's life in addition to complete control.)

One group is the obvious: those who were afflicted against their wills. Whether or not they understood what was happening to them, they were tormented and did not want to do the will of the devil.

> *And immediately there was in their synagogue a man with an unclean spirit. And he cried out, "What have you to do with us, Jesus of Nazareth? Have you come to destroy us? I know who you are—the Holy One of God." But Jesus rebuked him, saying, "Be silent, and come out of him!" And the unclean spirit, convulsing him and crying out with a loud voice, came out of him.* (Mark 1:23-26)

> *And behold, a Canaanite woman from that region came out and was crying, "Have mercy on me, O Lord, Son of David; my daughter is severely oppressed by a demon."* (Matthew 15:22)

The other group is perhaps not quite as obvious. It is those to whom Jesus was speaking in John 8:44.

> *You are of your father the devil, and your will is to do your father's desires.*

Who was this group?

It was the religious leaders.

Jesus said they *wanted* to do the devil's work.

Not every religious leader, of course. The Scriptures show that there were some, such as Nicodemus, who wanted to know Jesus and bow before Him.

But this, as well as several other Scriptures, indicate that there were—and are—respected religious leaders who have given themselves over to the devil. [108]

They are in the churches, even today. Men (and women) who actually *want* to do the devil's work are leading churches.

So what are we as Jesus-lovers and Jesus-followers to do?

The forces of evil are all around us, but as ambassadors of the Kingdom of God we do not need to fear. The power and authority of our Lord Jesus Christ are far greater.

An example of spiritual authority

A friend who was raised in a Reformed church told me she learned about her authority in Jesus Christ when she went to Bible school and studied spiritual warfare. Then she went on a mission trip to China. She wrote me this story:

> *The atmosphere in that part of China was the darkest place I have been in my life. A missionary who had previously been deep in Mongolia for ten years and had gone through indescribable hardships told me that she had never faced darkness like what dominated this Chinese city. In the four months leading to my hospitalization, I had been*

---

[108] See, for example, the references given in Chapter 14. There are also those who live in denial and deception, who are doing the devil's work without realizing it. That is not the group Jesus was talking to here.

18 – THE AUTHORITY WE HAVE IN JESUS CHRIST

experiencing heavy emotional struggles, physical exhaustion, and spiritual warfare. Every day was an intense battle. Physically, emotionally, and spiritually, everything seemed to climax when I got appendicitis.

When I was suffering agonizing pain the night before my emergency surgery, I had a demonic dream/vision of a serpent-being who was tormenting me. It was not just what looked like a snake; it was a real presence of a demonic being in my room. I commanded it away in the name of Jesus even though I had very little strength, and the infinite power of Jesus drove it away, immediately giving me peace.

If I had not learned at Bible school that I have that authority, I do not know what I would have done. Though I was going through intense physical suffering, my soul was fully at peace.

There is nothing like walking through a dark valley with Jesus to reveal the priceless beauty of His Light.[109]

This friend experienced a demon tormenting her, attacking her. This was not because of her sin, and she felt no shame about it.

She also didn't need to feel fear, because *she knew what to do*. She knew her authority in the Lord Jesus Christ and needed to command it away.

Knowing our delegated authority in Jesus Christ makes the difference, in a situation like that one, between *asking God for help* and *issuing a command*. This friend knew she could issue the command.

---

[109] Personal correspondence, January 2021, used by permission.

There are times when asking God for help isn't the best course of action. Sometimes the help is already there—and we just need to make use of it.

Because this problem isn't just in China. Demonic forces are at work all over the world, and in Western countries too.

What we need for this battle

We need freedom from abusive systems

Even if we're physically free, it might take a while to complete the "getting free." Those old voices can still be in our heads and hearts.

But if you want to walk in victory and authority, it's essential to keep working at separating the toxic from the true.

The further we can get from the lies of the abusers and their abusive systems—not just physically, but in our souls—the better we'll be able to see who we really are in Christ. And the more we'll be able to walk in victory over the powers of darkness.

We need to draw near to God

This doesn't mean we need to be flawless or sinless. It means our hearts are *truly His*. It means our hearts do not purposely harbor secret wickedness but are moving toward our Lord in faith, being drawn by His love.

This also means listening to the Holy Spirit, which is more than I can discuss here. But it is so important for those of us who love Jesus to learn to do, in order to grow in the Christian life to which He has called us.

We need to know the truth

This is not a physical battle to be waged in the power of the flesh.

We are in a *spiritual* battle, to be waged in the power of the *Spirit*.

> *For we do not wrestle against flesh and blood, but against the rulers, against the authorities, against the cosmic powers over this present darkness, against the spiritual forces of evil in the heavenly places.* (Ephesians 6:12)

When we understand who Jesus really is and who we really are, then we can begin to grasp the spiritual authority that we truly have been given in Him.

> *Blessed be the God and Father of our Lord Jesus Christ, who has blessed us in Christ with every spiritual blessing in the heavenly places, even as he chose us in him before the foundation of the world, that we should be holy and blameless before him.* (Ephesians 1:3-4)

That grounding in *who Jesus Christ really is* and *who you really are in Him*, and *how He works in and through you*—there is no substitute for that when it comes to spiritual warfare.

> *For in [Christ] the whole fullness of deity dwells bodily, and you have been filled in him, who is the head of all rule and authority.* (Colossians 2:9-10)

We need to learn the truth, deeply

You can read books on the topic, and you can listen to speakers. But humans, all of us, are fallible and can go astray.

The most reliable way to absorb the truth of God about these topics is to read the Bible for yourself, especially the New

Testament, since you are a New Covenant believer. Read it with a humble, searching heart, asking the Holy Spirit to open your eyes to more and more truth—about Him, about yourself, about the world, and about the spirit realm. Continue to seek Him and know Him through His Word and His Spirit. Reading Scripture for yourself is paramount.

Know Jesus. He teaches you who He is through the Scriptures and through His Spirit.[110]

> *For God, who said, "Let light shine out of darkness," has shone in our hearts to give the light of the knowledge of the glory of God in the face of Jesus Christ. But we have this treasure in jars of clay, to show that the surpassing power belongs to God and not to us.* (2 Corinthians 4:6-7)
>
> *My sheep hear my voice, and I know them, and they follow me.* (John 10:27)

Know yourself. You can learn who you are in Jesus Christ through the Scriptures. But sometimes you may need some help fully understanding what happened to you in your past and how that has affected you, including your view of yourself and God and your understanding of truth. Sometimes you may need help understanding things such as brain science and history (your own, your family, and more). Sometimes you may need help

---

[110] A wise friend said, "When the Spirit and the Word seem to contradict each other, we do need to face into that, to find out where truth lies. Often the truth is that we have misunderstood the Word, or how it applies. Nathanael and Peter were two who had to decide whether to believe the Spirit of God, when what he said to them seemed to contradict the Word of God. The issue is not which is more to be trusted, the Spirit or the Word. The issue goes back to this: Are our hearts truly His? And are our hearts open to the truth he wants to reveal to us? The extent to which our heart is open is the extent to which God can show us where we've misunderstood the Word, or missed the Spirit, or both - and can show us his Word by his Spirit, and reveal his Spirit in his Word."

grasping these truths not only in your intellect, but in your experience.[111]

Understand the spiritual battle. We are at war, as the Scriptures tell us and as experience shows. The adversary is doomed, but he wants to deceive, rob, destroy, confuse, oppress, and take down as many people as possible. He'll use a variety of tactics to do it.[112]

Jesus said in John 10:10,

> *The thief comes only to steal and kill and destroy. I came that they may have life and have it abundantly.*

The answer to the denial and deception of the enemy comes in untwisting the lies and knowing the truth. Truth leads to understanding. Greater understanding leads to deeper awareness of truth. Greater awareness of truth exposes error and helps others out of their ignorance and confusion.

> *And I heard a loud voice in heaven, saying, "Now the salvation and the power and the kingdom of our God and the authority of his Christ have come, for the accuser of our brothers has been thrown down, who accuses them day and night before our God. And they have conquered him by the blood of the Lamb and by the word of their testimony, for they loved not their lives even unto death."* (Revelation 12:10-11)

---

[111] Though this may be going a bit far afield from the discussion of our authority in Jesus Christ, I believe it's an important point: Becoming more and more free from the effects of trauma, especially childhood trauma, can help enable us to come into the fullness of who we are in Christ, which is important for us to be able to fully embrace the authority He has given us.

[112] The variety of tactics the enemy uses is the subject of many books, but a few are denial, deception, doubt, confusion, fear, and promises of power, pleasure, or fame.

We need to distinguish spiritual authority in Jesus Christ from magic

Some Christians who lack understanding may want to use Christian words, phrases, symbols, activities, or items to affect the spirit realm in a "magical" way, but this idea comes from paganism. The Adversary can use this ignorance to draw people into confusion, including Christ-followers.

For example, some Christians have believed that practicing "grave soaking" would give them the authority of the dead person whose grave they lie on. Some have thought that making the sign of the cross would give them authority against demons.

But spiritual warfare isn't about some physical action we take in this physical realm. It is about spiritual action in the spirit realm. Spiritual warfare is a holy undertaking.

Acts 19 tells the story of seven young men who thought they could cast out demons by copying Paul. After all, they had heard his words. But the demons responded, "I know Jesus, and I know Paul, but who are you?"

Obviously, it was the personal relationship with Jesus Christ that mattered, and truly acting as His representative. Not simply a set of "magic words."

We have authority available to us always when we come against the enemy through the Lord Jesus Christ. This means not just by saying His Name, but by being one of His sheep and a child of His Kingdom, as the previous chapter describes.

We need to know what our spiritual authority is for and what it's not for

Sadly, because of the times—or maybe better, because of human nature—I have to make this part crystal clear.

18 – THE AUTHORITY WE HAVE IN JESUS CHRIST

Your authority is not about power or pleasure in this physical realm. (That is one of the devil's chief deceptions.)

It is about the Kingdom of God.

Your authority is not to claim something you want for your own comfort.

It is authority against the realm of evil.

Your authority is not about accomplishing your own will.

It is authority to accomplish God's will that He has stated in Scripture.

Your authority is not to declare particular events that should take place here on earth.

It is the authority to stand against demonic spirits as we do our work for the Kingdom of our Lord Jesus Christ in His spiritual Kingdom (not a physical one).

You have been given no authority over God. You haven't even been given spiritual authority over other people.

The power and strength God wants us to have is *in the spiritual realm*. Against the *spiritual forces of evil*.

Your authority means you can stand against evil spirits that come against you personally, for example, in your thought life.[113]

It also means you can stand in authority against evil spirits that are binding another person who needs to be freed.

Some time ago, a woman I was working with in my prayer ministry was unquestionably demonized. That is, she saw the demons, she heard the demons, and sometimes the demons wrote messages to me through her.

---

[113] This video series from Deeper Walk International "Understanding the Wounded Heart" explains more about this.
https://www.youtube.com/playlist?list=PLrQfrwC_jtCCSaKSB2FH9ol-wKhm6xg7wi

Her situation was a complicated one that wasn't a once-and-done affair, but every time the demons manifested, I quietly responded with a command to leave. (Except sometimes I answered their emails.)

There came a point in her healing process when—though it was a while before they completely left her alone—they stopped using her to try to threaten me. Our progress was step by step until she came to Jesus and learned to exercise her authority in Jesus herself. Eventually she was completely freed.

Step by step

Approach mysteries humbly

Sometimes when people command evil spirits out and away for an afflicted person, but nothing changes, they blame the afflicted one for lack of faith. But they have no authority to do that. This is how spiritual warfare can become spiritual abuse.

Also, if you seek to stand in your authority in regard to an issue in your own life, but you haven't experienced breakthrough, you don't want to shame yourself. (Abuse survivors can often be harder on themselves than anyone else.)

In either case, you do have recourse. You can come boldly before the throne of God to humbly ask Him what is standing in the way of freedom and victory.

> *Since then we have a great high priest who has passed through the heavens, Jesus, the Son of God, let us hold fast our confession. For we do not have a high priest who is unable to sympathize with our weaknesses, but one who in every respect has been tempted as we are, yet without sin. Let us then with confidence draw near to the throne of grace, that we may receive mercy and find grace to help in time of need.* (Hebrews 4:14-16)

There may be some very complicated situations or issues you don't yet see. As a couple of examples, when a person has suffered lifelong abuse there can be much shame as well as much confusion, both of which are powerful tools of the devil. In the life of a satanic ritual abuse survivor, there may be spiritual binding that is not the person's fault at all, but it may take some time and much spiritual discernment to untangle.

We continue to seek our Lord through His Spirit. We hope and expect His good answers. *Because we know we're on the winning side.* We humble ourselves under the mighty hand of God. And we stand confident in Him.

> *God opposes the proud but gives grace to the humble. Submit yourselves therefore to God. Resist the devil, and he will flee from you.* (James 4:6b-7)

The ability to resist the devil is preceded by submitting to God. When we have come to Him in humility and asked Him to take charge in our lives, confessing our sins and asking for His infilling, then we will be able to stand against the devil and his minions and know they will flee.

Practice your authority

If we don't recognize and stand on our faith-filled authority in the spiritual realm—the realm of the Kingdom Jesus talked about in Luke 12:32—then we'll suffer from the "flaming darts" of the enemy *without even understanding what's going on.*

> *In all circumstances take up the shield of faith, with which you can extinguish all the flaming darts of the evil one.* (Ephesians 6:16)

I once fought a very personal spiritual battle, in which I became entangled and enveloped in demonic darkness. It was weeks before I finally recognized it as a demonic attack. For over a year

I sought God through the Scriptures, and the Word came alive to me even as I was still in the darkness, still feeling like I was being held underwater. I began to see Jesus more fully for who He really is. Though I didn't understand yet about making *commands*, finally one day I made a *declaration*. I cried out loud from the depths of my being, "Jesus, You are all my righteousness! You are my complete salvation! You are my only Hope!"

I knew, deep down, He was my only hope. And indeed, He did deliver me and prepare me to wage warfare not just for myself, but for others as well.[114]

Once you're willing to face and fight the battles in your own life, once you come out on the other side of those battles victorious, the Lord will bring you to others who need help. They in turn can then be brought to a place of freedom and understanding. Then they too will be able to exercise their spiritual authority in Jesus Christ.

In my personal ministry work with individuals, we address all the expected topics of truth, lies, sin, shame, trauma, and so forth (and yes, we address forgiveness). But in some cases the person I'm working with clearly is or might be hindered by evil spirits and want to be free. Sometimes in this work I may discern possible hindrances in the spirit realm. In cases like these, there is no need to be afraid, because Jesus is far greater than any evil spirits. There is no reason to respond by raising my voice, because demons aren't hard of hearing.

Instead, I give a quiet command such as this one, just as I would pray a quiet prayer. It is done recognizing that our Lord

---

[114] This story is told more fully in my book *Prayer Armor for Defense against the Enemy's Flaming Darts*, Pennycress Publishing, 2019, pp. 23-24.

18 – THE AUTHORITY WE HAVE IN JESUS CHRIST

Jesus is the ultimate authority over the evil and knows exactly what to do.[115]

> *In the Name and by the authority of the Lord Jesus Christ, the only begotten Son of God, as His daughter and representative, I command any evil spirits that may be hindering this work today to be gone from here and go to the feet of Jesus, for Him to do with as He will.*

Often, then, the person I'm working with and I will find that the confusion or fog or darkness has lifted, and we can move forward.

Align our desires and will with God's desire and will

In the first *Untwisting Scriptures* book, in the chapters about "yielding rights," I wrote about the importance of our desires aligning with the will of God. I said that though genuine *rights* cannot ever be yielded, our *desires* must always be yielded to the Lord, aligned with His will.[116]

I want to say the same thing here, but with a different emphasis. Some Christians, when they learn about the authority we have in the spirit realm, believe that God will yield to their desires. Nothing could be further from the truth, and a path such as this one will lead to evil.

Rather than assuming that God's will is going to align with our desires, we look to Him, attuning our hearts to Him, to align *our desires, our wills,* with the will of God.

---

[115] The larger picture of helping a demonized person get free from evil spirits involves more than can be discussed here.

[116] Rebecca Davis, *Untwisting Scriptures that were used to tie you up, gag you, and tangle your mind.* Justice Keepers Publishing, 2016, p. 32.

How we can know we're on the right track

Spiritual authority that is aligned with the will and desires of God . . .

- ➢ shows love for others and helps them find healing.
- ➢ exposes evil.
- ➢ leads those who are in spiritual bondage into freedom from sin and shame.
- ➢ leads to wholeness and strength for the spiritually wounded and oppressed.
- ➢ brings souls into God's Kingdom.
- ➢ helps strengthen those souls for spiritual battle.
- ➢ glorifies God by showing His majesty and His heart of love.

Spiritual authority from God begins and ends with His love, the love that Jesus held up as paramount in Matthew 22:35-40.

> *And one of [the Pharisees, a student of the Mosaic law], asked [Jesus] a question to test him. "Teacher, which is the great commandment in the Law?"*
>
> *And he said to him, "You shall love the Lord your God with all your heart and with all your soul and with all your mind. This is the great and first commandment.*
>
> *And a second is like it: You shall love your neighbor as yourself. On these two commandments depend all the Law and the Prophets."*

In John 13:34 Jesus made it even more clear:

> *A new commandment I give to you, that you love one another: just as I have loved you, you also are to love one another.*

Spiritual authority from Jesus Christ is never simply a display of power. It is filled with and fueled by love, love for God and love for others. Always.

If it is not, then it will become simply one more tool for the devil.

> *If I have prophetic powers, and understand all mysteries and all knowledge, and if I have all faith, so as to remove mountains, but have not love, I am nothing.* (1 Corinthians 3:2)

But when love is the core and the goal, we will see our Holy Lord Jesus Christ, the God of glory, lifted up and exalted. We will see souls joyfully brought into His Kingdom, into close relationship with Him, which He delights to give to His flock.

This is the aim and joy of the Christian life.

Always.

Appendix A

Examining the Matriarchs of Patriarchy

IN HER 1985 book *The Way Home: Beyond Feminism Back to Reality,* thirty-year-old Mary Pride slams her readers from the start with twisted Scripture, twisted facts, and a terrifying view of a world in which all things evil lie ahead if Christian women do not embrace their "biblical" role of making their lives all, and only, about family and home.

She suggests that any woman who steps out of this patriarchal view of "women's sphere" is on her way to embracing the most radical and godless feminism, totalitarianism, and Antichrist. Inevitably, such women will destroy their families, and destroy society too.

Any woman who is frustrated or unhappy trying to stay "in her place," she teaches, has in fact been robbed of her role (by the greatest con since the serpent deceived Eve). And Mary Pride affirms: All women will be happy and fulfilled— and will train up children who are successful and godly, and so will positively impact all society—if they will not just "stay home," but rather will get busy working at home, teaching their children and making sure their husband is the one in charge.

The author of the following article, a woman whose life was influenced by the matriarchs of patriarchy, is a stay-at-home mother who homeschools her children. She exposes the wrongs of the movement not because she is opposed to staying at home and homeschooling (she loves them, as I do), but because Mary Pride and others held them out as "the answers" to life's problems when they are not.

The influence of *The Way Home*

Mary Pride's argument

> *When women were stuck at home in the fifties with only their birth control pills and dishwashers for company, no wonder they went crazy! If God really wanted us to live that way, we could swallow our frustrations and do it. But since it was an abnormal lifestyle, frustration led to rebellion.*[117]

Mary Pride rails against the ideology of feminism, setting up the straw man of bored 1950s housewives who "went crazy."

In her book, Pride outlines that feminism brought about the rejection of children, which caused women to become "frustrated" and then stray from God's plan for their lives.

Yes, an "abnormal lifestyle" not based in reality can lead to frustration (though, as an observation, birth control was not readily available in the 1950s, and an average housewife did not have a dishwasher in her home until many years later).

But frustration does not necessarily lead to rebellion. Rules without relationship, however, can lead to rebellion of one form or another.

---

[117] Mary Pride, *The Way Home: Beyond Feminism, Back to Reality*, Crossway Publications, 1985, p 166.

APPENDIX A: THE MATRIARCHS OF PATRIARCHY

Using Bible verses, Mary Pride offers her solution to the "frustration" caused by feminism, developing a stay-at-home doctrine for the Christian wife and mother.

Was the reasoning of this doctrine sound reasoning?

And now, 35 years later, what can we learn from it?

Thirty-five years to examine

When Mary Pride wrote *The Way Home*, she was looking back 30 years, the span of her life at the time, to her mother's generation.

And now, Mary Pride's generation is the generation of my own mother. The women who followed Mary Pride, in my mother's generation, were the first wave of the modern Stay-at-Home movement. So, like her, I am looking back.

I am analyzing patterns of lifestyle choices of beliefs, to see how we can make necessary changes and keep from repeating mistakes that can lead to hurting others.

Who were those 1950s women anyway?

Mary Pride described an "abnormal lifestyle" of the 1950s that led to frustration that led to rebellion.

This was the era of my grandmothers, both of whom are the hardest working women *at home* that I have ever known. My mother's mother was the wife of a dairy farmer, working sunup to sundown in all manner of household and outdoor chores. After my mother went to college, my grandmother worked at an office job for a number of years. My father's mother was a seamstress, a homemaker, and a gardener; she worked hard all summer long canning food for the winter months.

Both of these women put their children first in raising them, and cared for their own mothers in their old age. My grandmothers are Christians who love Jesus and love their husbands. They are both eighty-six years old and have both served God alongside their husbands for sixty-seven years.

These are the "women of the fifties" that thirty-year-old Mary Pride disparaged.

Even though for the most part their lives modeled what Mary Pride taught, my grandmothers would not have subscribed to her teachings, simply because they would not claim either feminist or anti-feminist doctrines in support of the way they lived their lives. They were level-headed, minding their own business and attending to their own work. They simply lived for Jesus.

The "homeworking" doctrine

A new agenda centering around the home instead of Jesus

Through promotion on James Dobson's radio program and word-of-mouth recommendations, woman to woman, Mary Pride's book became a best seller. (By and large, the husbands were not the ones promoting this book or these teachings. It was primarily the women.)

In reaction to feminist ideologies, Mary Pride and others[118] developed a new agenda with its own mantras, under the guise of "obedience to God." *The Way Home* claimed that in order to be more spiritual and godly, women must live their lives completely centered around their homes, their husband and children, home schooling, and home activities.

---

[118] Nancy Pearcey, Edith Schaeffer, Susan Wise Bauer, and Inge Cannon, along with Mary Pride of course, were arguably some of the most influential women leaders of the stay-at-home and patriarchy movement of the late 1980s through the 1990s. But how did they get to be authorities on homeschooling, home-making lifestyles and child-rearing? Who appointed them?

There was no mention of centering their lives on Jesus. The only "Biblical" response to feminism was that all women must go home and stay home.

This was the beginning of what would become the Homeschool Quiverfull Patriarchy Movement, a movement that taught doctrines of authoritarian dominance over women and children.

Contradictions in The Way Home

In calling women "back home," Mary Pride influenced women to become dependent upon others. She also created a good deal of confusion with her contradictory statements.

Listen to your elders ... or not

With the publication of *The Way Home*, Mary Pride became an almost instant authority on anti-feminism dogma, homemaking, and homeschooling. With a fascinating bit of irony, she exhorted her peers to listen to the older women, while she herself, at the age of 30, was teaching them.

How did she justify this, when she had been living this lifestyle for only five years and her children were still small?

Submit to your husband ... or not

After having written several chapters on why and how a woman must be submissive, Pride, perhaps without realizing it, presents an abusive husband.

> *Women today are being pushed, in some cases with the church's blessing, into working outside the home whether they want to or not.*
>
> *The culprit, in most cases, is the husband. Suddenly all the articles about working wives click, and he gets dollar signs in his eyes. "$10,000 a year on the hoof! I could buy a vacation cabin with that!" So he brutally forces his wife to put the*

> children in day care, forbids her to become pregnant, and sends her out into a job she does not want.[119]

She goes on to say that a wife must quit her job . . . but get her husband's approval.

> *So the very first step is to win your husband's consent. ... A submissive wife doesn't just force her will on her husband. She explains to him how what she is asking fits into his goals."*[120]

But instead of "his goals" (or "her goals"), in a truly mutual Christian marriage a husband and wife will have mutual goals. They will discuss, pray, and work together to achieve those mutual goals.

Each man and woman is created with a God-given conscience. In a loving marriage relationship, submitting to one another in love, a husband and wife respect and honor one another in their relationships with Jesus and ability to listen to the Holy Spirit.

Why did young women flock to it?

They were looking for answers

If a woman in the 1950s had "gone crazy," could there be another reason besides "frustration leading to rebellion" as Pride says? Broad sweeping generalizations are harmful and hurtful; we would do well to ask what were the deeper questions that permeated the hearts of women and offer a loving response to the questions of their souls.

So I have done the same.

---

[119] Ibid., p 161.

[120] Ibid., pp 211-212.

I have spoken with mothers who homeschooled their children who tell how Mary Pride was the greatest influential voice at the time and how she led them into following the patriarchal lifestyle.

Why did so many women embrace these teachings so readily?

Many of the women who have spoken to me of their early days in homeschooling were seeking answers to the deep questions in their lives. A number of them were struggling with depression, anxiety, instability, fear of failure, sadness, uncertainty, or grief. These are characteristics of women who have suffered.

They tended to be lacking in confidence. In many cases they did not know their own minds. (Or if they did, they were under the control of others and were unable to find freedom from that mental and emotional bondage.)

The eager audience—Christian wives, mothers, and daughters—were trying to do better than the generation prior, and in many cases were trying to do better than they themselves had done in their previous "wild" years.

They desired a new way of life. They wanted to know and follow the truth, for themselves and their families. The stay-at-home message sounded so good, so right, so Biblical.

These young wives did what they believed was right, with an attitude of submission. Conditioned to put themselves aside and "lose their identity," they sought to find purpose and fulfillment in homelife and childbearing.

It can be easy to unwittingly buy into an offer that promises fulfillment, especially when it is wrapped in spiritual jargon.

They began leading when the husband wouldn't

I have known many homeschooling families. Only a small percentage of them began homeschooling with a patriarchal vision for their family because the *husband* made the decision to do so.

In a very high percentage, it was the *wives* who followed the leaders of the patriarchal teachings and adopted them for their families. Seeking meaning and fruitfulness in their lives, many women soaked up this new decision-making process and lifestyle.

Perhaps they didn't realize it was a formula, as a number of us who have lived through that formula do now.

Wanting them to take charge, wives encouraged their husbands to read and listen to the men in positions of leadership in the Patriarchal community who *were* taking control over their households. Men such as John Thompson, Jonathan Lindvall, Matthew Chapman, Phil Lancaster, Douglas Wilson, Douglas Phillips, S.M. Davis, Geoff Botkin and R.C. Sproul, Jr, garnered support from *wives* across the United States who desperately wanted their own husbands to be like these men.

The personal testimonies of dozens of women who shared with me are very similar: their husbands were not leading, so they took the reins. A wife urged her husband to adopt the teachings and convictions espoused by the stay-at-home movement, leading the family into new precepts of beliefs and practices, until the husband gave in and acquiesced.

As an article on the Quivering Daughters website explored, the number of female bloggers promoting patriarchy far exceeded the number of male bloggers on the topic.[121]

The wife waited expectantly for her husband to begin leading. She would speak to others of her submission to and respect of his authority over her life.

Yet in many cases these husbands were passive (and in some cases they were addicted to pornography). Did these husbands

---

[121] E. Stephen Burnett, "Bill Gothard and Patriarchy: Re-routed Feminism?" Quivering Daughters, February 2011. https://quiveringdaughters.blogspot.com/2011/02/bill-gothard-and-patriarchy-re-routed.html

hold to the "homelife" practices as their own? Or merely to keep peace with their wives?

What did it lead to?

Following the leader led to ignoring the Holy Spirit

Attempting to support her "coming home will make everything right again" position with out-of-context passages from God's Word, Mary Pride listed rules of conduct and submission for wives and mothers who desired to live for God.

But where was the resounding encouragement to study the life of Jesus and listen to Him? After all, wasn't this intended to be a *Christian* response to a secular agenda? Yet, where did these books and teachings encourage listening to the leading of the Holy Spirit?

Women who desired a more fruitful purpose in their lives were instructed to soak up the teachings of other interpreters of the Bible, rather than listening to the Spirit of God for themselves. In these teachings, the reader was not encouraged to talk to or hear from Jesus and follow His guidance for their daily lives. Rather, they flocked to others who had answers to their questions about fulfillment and purpose.

A few women have admitted to me that when they did not fully agree with the interpretations of child-bearing, homelife, or submission, they were guilted and peer-pressured into adopting the principles as their own. It was a mantra of, "Just obey what we tell you is the right way to live, and don't question those who know better than you do. We know what is most Biblical, and you must submit to it." Independent thinking was squelched under the control of "authorities."

When a herd flocks to popular teachings that remove the need to listen to the Lord and make wise Spirit-led decisions, this a dangerous road indeed.

> *Enter through the narrow gate. For wide is the gate and broad is the road that leads to destruction and many enter through it.* (Matthew 7:13)

A different kind of bondage

If women were looking for godliness through the "homelife" movement, they were sold a bill of goods. A life centered around home-making is not necessarily spiritual or godly.

The lives and choices of feminists were used to bring judgment upon the lives and choices of women who wanted to follow Jesus, who desired to know the truth.

Teachers like Mary Pride encouraged women to submit to their husbands and church leaders almost without qualification, as long as it followed her "homeworking" agenda. Women were encouraged to submit to *men* and *doctrines*, rather than Jesus.

Following manmade (or woman-made) rules, believing them to be the leading of the Spirit of God, many women eventually found themselves in chains of a different kind of bondage.

This new movement, instead of providing the promised fulfilment, often led to spiritual confusion and sometimes even spiritual abuse. Instead of providing the promised freedom, it often resulted in a kind of bondage for both women and children, in some cases literally.

The missing ingredient in promoting this new movement of telling women they must return home? Real love. The true love of Jesus was missing.

We each have the responsibility to make decisions for our lives based on the love of Jesus, with Jesus having authority over our lives. Jesus stated in Matthew 28:18, "All authority has been given to me in heaven and on earth." Husbands and wives are to be submitted to Him together.

Well-meaning women with the heart to love God and do good to others were often led unwittingly into the enslavement of spiritual abuse.

Some husbands/fathers became very controlling when that was not in their nature, because they thought that was what God wanted from them. Some husbands/fathers loved exerting their power and control. But some remained passive, allowing their wives to lead.

Some of these wives and mothers would then go on to become spiritually abusive themselves, dogmatically condemning other wives and daughters who did not adopt these doctrines of homemaking as described in *The Way Home*. Some eventually became controlling and dominating in the home, especially because of the peer pressure to measure up to the standard of the "godly home."

This last group, along with well-known leaders like Mary Pride, became the Matriarchs of Patriarchy.

These chains of spiritual abuse were passed on to me and my generation who were homeschooled in the stay-at-home "Biblical Patriarchy" movement.

Observations from a friend

Here is a testimony from a friend who was raised in a family that was heavily influenced by Mary Pride:

> *The fear growing up in our home was palpable. Unspoken, perhaps, but very present and very real. The all-too-familiar "sex, drugs and rock-n-roll" line made an appearance here and there in conversations, of course, explaining the "sheltered" mentality they adopted along with their fellow Homeschooling Movement peers.*

They essentially created their own subculture, following the blueprint laid down by Mary Pride and her ilk, shielding their children from the evils of mainstream society (or so they thought). They started their own home churches and home school support groups; they rarely let us play with public school kids lest we be contaminated.

Why the fearful paralysis of our parents' generation? And what are we, the next generation, to do about it?

The horrors they saw in the world were real; so heinous that they cannot bring themselves to tell us everything, even to this day, thirty-plus years later. Their concerns were legitimate. Their fear was valid. But like so many snake-oil charlatans of bygone eras, the Mary Prides of our mothers' era took advantage of the fearful, well-meaning concern of our parents. They offered a formula: "Follow this (and buy my books!) and your children will be guaranteed safe! They will grow up to be wise and godly and will pass on your legacy to the next generation!"

Hearing the Holy Spirit requires listening and patience. When Elijah hid in a cave in the side of a mountain (for a valid reason: Jezebel was out to kill him again), he waited on the Lord. There was a great windstorm, then a terrible earthquake, then a massive fire. But God was not in any of these things. Finally, Elijah heard a gentle whisper: the Spirit of God telling him what he should do. "Call upon the Lord and He will answer you."

It's okay to hide in a cave for a season. But may we never stop listening for that gentle Voice of Jesus, whispering on the breeze and into our souls.

Where we are today

When the "back to the home" movement works

Working in the home, homeschooling your children, gardening, making bread, all are good things, and caring for your family is essential. Home can be a place of life and love and joy and peace.

But that will be the case not because we follow rules to do life the way someone has told us to. But because we love the Lord first and then love others as we love ourselves.

That needs to be true of both parents, even ones in which "the father has the final word." The home needs to be filled with love. And in a home like this, when the parents teach the children to love God and love others, they will be teaching by example.

Courageous women today

If Mary Pride's book hadn't been part of the equation, if patriarchal teachings had been promoted only by men and not by a young woman, the doctrine of patriarchy might not have caught on with these hopeful new mothers the way it did.

I have heard from women who initially bought into these doctrines and teachings espoused by Mary Pride, et al., and have realized in recent years that they were sold a bill of goods. They have changed their minds after many years of struggle with truth and reality.

Scores of the marriages that were characterized by the doctrines laid out in *The Way Home* have been fraught with emotional trauma, domestic violence, child abuse, and spiritual abuse.

These wives and mamas could not foresee how this belief system would backfire twenty, thirty years later with their own children, or the tremendous suffering that would become a part of their lives as a result.

But coming out of that wreckage, strong, courageous, honest women today who walk with Jesus have been able to look forward with hope and conviction, having learned from the past.

These women have resolved instead to listen to the Holy Spirit. They have turned away from man's word and turned to the truths of God's Word.

With compassion, kindness, and a Jesus kind of love, they have decided to follow Jesus. There is hope for our souls in no one but Him.

APPENDIX B

Further Questions and Answers on "Children Obey Your Parents"

I RECEIVED SOME questions on my blog post of "(Adult) Children Obey Your Parents"[122] (chapter 8 of this book). Select questions and comments are included here.

Question about "teknon"

> I looked up all the times "teknon" was used and it does refer to adult "children" some of the time, as in Acts 13:33, 2 Timothy 1:2 and 1 Peter 3:6. Would you comment on these?

My response

> Acts 13:32-33 "We tell you the good news: What God promised our ancestors he has fulfilled for us, their children, by raising up Jesus. As it is written in the second

---

[122] https://heresthejoy.com/2017/10/adult-children-obey-your-parents-part-2-for-adults-raised-in-patriarchy/

> *Psalm: "'You are my son; today I have become your father.'"*

There was a very strong generational bond among the Jews in the sense that one generation depended on the prophecies, promises, and other Scriptures given to the previous generations. This would be true for them even as adults, though as adults they were responsible before God to follow Jesus Christ themselves without the previous generations telling them how it was to be done. In fact, they, the current generation, were now telling the older generation how to follow God.

> 1 Peter 3:5-6 *"For this is the way the holy women of the past who put their hope in God used to adorn themselves. They submitted themselves to their own husbands, like Sarah, who obeyed Abraham and called him her lord. You are her daughters if you do what is right and do not give way to fear."*

This is referring to a spiritual relationship, in the sense that when you do what is right you can say, "I'm a daughter of Sarah," whether or not you're physically descended from her.

> 2 Timothy 1:1-2 *"Paul, an apostle of Christ Jesus by the will of God, in keeping with the promise of life that is in Christ Jesus, To Timothy, my dear son: Grace, mercy and peace from God the Father and Christ Jesus our Lord."*

There is definitely a father-son bond here, even though it's a spiritual one. It's a good example of the use of this word in the case of an adult "son," because you can see from the letters to Timothy that Paul (as Timothy's spiritual father) didn't expect to control Timothy's actions, choices, decisions, and thoughts, but expected Timothy to conduct himself wisely led by the Spirit of God in matters of the churches, with the guidelines Paul was laying out for him from afar.

APPENDIX B: QUESTIONS ON "CHILDREN OBEY YOUR PARENTS"

Question about "bring them up"

> I noticed that the phrase "bring them up" from Ephesians 6 is the same as the word "nourishes" from Ephesians 5:29. What is your take on that, and how does it fit with your explanation?

My response

> Ephesians 5:28-29 *"In this same way, husbands ought to love their wives as their own bodies. He who loves his wife loves himself. After all, no one ever hated their own body, but they feed and care for their body, just as Christ does the church— for we are members of his body."*

This passage is about an adult caring for his own physical body, which becomes a person's own responsibility once he becomes mature. In the same way, in the spiritual realm, which is the context of Ephesians 6:3, when children are young they need someone else to nurture or care for them. When they are adults, they can and should nurture or care for themselves.

Clarification in regard to the proper use of the Greek language

When I worked on this article, I asked for help on the Greek from my friend Sam Powell (a pastor and blogger at www.myonlycomfort.com who is also a Greek and Hebrew scholar).

He argued that the meaning of Greek words is found not primarily in lexicons but in context, saying, "The words 'obey' and 'children' mean almost exactly in Greek what they mean in English, nuanced, and varied, and understood in context. . . . The exegesis of this passage isn't determined by the lexicon, since the words are basic and common. The exegesis is on context and in the proportion of faith. In other words, anyone reading this without an agenda would understand immediately what was meant."[123]

As an example, if I stood at the edge of a crowd of people of all ages and called, "Children! Come for lessons!" then some younger teenagers might puzzle over whether or not they were included in my call, but adults would know they weren't included. This is basically what the apostle Paul was doing—speaking to a large group of people of all ages and expecting them to understand who he was delineating.

Bible commentators through ages past have understood this term in this part of Scripture to mean young children, not adults, and didn't even bother trying to sort it out because to them the meaning was self-evident.

Sam Powell again: "When God said, 'Children, obey your parents,' he also said, 'Let no one again place you under bondage.' And 'Woe to the one who puts his trust in man.' And 'There is one mediator between God and man, the man Christ Jesus.' So God certainly did not mean that a father has the absolute right over the souls of his children, telling them what to believe and how to believe it. That only belongs to Jesus."[124]

Sam concludes with a comment about authority: "In my experience, those who have argued with me about the father's absolute right over his children and wife, based on these kinds of arguments, never submit to any authority other than themselves."[125]

Of course I don't know if this is the case in any of the parents you know, but this has been his experience.

---

[123] Comment on Here's the Joy "(Adult) children obey your parents? For adults raised in patriarchy," October 2017. https://her-esthejoy.com/2017/10/adult-children-obey-your-parents-part-2-for-adults-raised-in-patriarchy/

[124] Ibid.

[125] Ibid.

APPENDIX B: QUESTIONS ON "CHILDREN OBEY YOUR PARENTS"

Comment in regard to the pain felt by the controlling parent

> *I am well aware of the implications of taking a stand. When I think of it, when I see the pain in my father's eyes over my 4 siblings that have left, when I consider the good times and how much I love (and like) my dad (out of all 6 of us, I probably have the best relationship with him, although I can't share very deep heart issues), when I know that this may end our relationship, it tears my heart.*

My response

No matter what happens–whether you stay or go–there will be pain, and not just yours. Your father's too. It's not good for *him* for his children to continue to follow his every whim all his life. The best life for *him* will be for you to find a life of love and service for the Lord outside of himself.

Response from another reader

> *You mention how sad your father is about those who have "left" your family. It is one thing to be sad for those who have left following Christ, it is another thing to be sad for those who have left following him.*
>
> *Many well-intentioned fathers/husbands influenced by the patriarchal movement have made themselves the popes of their families. No one is allowed to think for themselves or hold interpretations outside of the father's. I know this may sound harsh, but the truth is that this is pure heresy, no matter how well-intentioned or "loving."*
>
> *One doctrine that really helped me to make this clear in my mind is the doctrine of the priesthood of the individual believer. This came to the forefront of Christian belief*

especially in the Reformation when many believers broke away from the Catholic Church and asserted their rights to believe as their own consciences were directed by Scripture. Please, do your own research on this—and let the truth set your heart free.[126]

A thought from one considering stepping away from her patriarchal family

My greatest fear is to not honor my Heavenly Father. When I think of that, I am quite willing to lay down my earthly relationship if need be.

---

[126] Comment on Here's the Joy "(Adult) children obey your parents? For adults raised in patriarchy," October 2017. https://heresthejoy.com/2017/10/adult-children-obey-your-parents-part-2-for-adults-raised-in-patriarchy/

Scripture Index

Genesis
19   p 46
24   p 45
29   p 46
34   p 23, p 47 footnote
38   p 46

Exodus
2:15-22   p 46
12:48-49   p 49
19:3-6   p 49
24:1-8   p 49
28:1-3   p 49
34:27-28   p 49

Numbers
30   p 25 footnote, pp 41-43, 46-47, 51

Deuteronomy
18:15-19   p 121

Judges
11:30-39   p 45

1 Samuel
15:23a   pp 80, 93
15:23   p 90
16:14   p 92
18   p 46

1 Chronicles
25:5-6   p 45

Nehemiah
3:12   p 45

Psalms

2	p 201
65:9-13	p 110
127:3-5	p 20
145:18	p 109
147:7-8	p 110

Proverbs

31	p 42

Isaiah

1:4	p 13 footnote, p 32 footnote
40	pp 161-165
55:7	p 32
55:10-11	p 110
62:11-12	p 165

Jeremiah

1:16	p 13 footnote, p 32 footnote
2:12-13	pp 13, 30, p 32 footnote
2:17, 19	p 13 footnote, p 32 footnote
3:12-13	p 33
5:3, 7, 19	p 13 footnote, p 32 footnote
5:30-31	p 130
8:5	p 13 footnote, p 32 footnote
14:14	p 130
17:13	p 13 footnote, p 32 footnote
19:4	p 13 footnote, p 32 footnote
22:9	p 13 footnote, p 32 footnote
31:31-34	p 50
35:15	p 32 footnote
36:3-7	p 32 footnote

Ezekiel

34	p 131

Daniel

1	p 80

APPENDIX B: QUESTIONS ON "CHILDREN OBEY YOUR PARENTS"

Micah
3:5   p 131

Matthew
5:45   p 110
7:13   p 195
7:15-16   p 131
8:5-10   pp 85-86
8:9   p 80
9:18-25   p 45
11:28-30   p 76
14:3-12   p 46
15:7-9   p 131
15:22   pp 171 - 172
16:6   p 155
19:29   p 74
20:25-26   p 29
20:25-28   p 140
22:35-40   p 184
22:37   p 29
23   pp 131, 155
23:2-3a   p 155
23:8-12   p 123
23:13   p 159
24:11   p 132
26:27-28   p 49
27   pp 158-159
27:20   p 136
28:18   pp 75, 167, 196

Mark
1:23-26   p 171
9:50   p 70
10:24   p 67
10:29-30   p 74
13:22   p 132
14:65   p 157

Luke
2:19	p 82
2:46-52	p 82
2:52	p 80
12:32	pp 75, 166, 169, 182
14:26	pp 74-75
18-29-30	p 74
22:19-20	p 48
22:25-26	p 139
22:53	p 159
22:63-65	p 157
24:45	p 43

John
3:11, 23	p 70
7:22	p 49
7:37-39	p 76
8:12	p 114
8:44	p 171
10:10	p 177
10:27	pp 73, 176
13:34	p 185
13:34-35	p 70
14:17, 26	p 44
16:13	p 44

Acts
2:29	p 5
5:29	pp 29, 61, 63
5:36	p 136
5:37	p 136
5:40	p 135
12	p 71
13:32-33	pp 201-202
13:43	p 134
14:16-17	p 110
14:19	p 136
15:22	p 139

APPENDIX B: QUESTIONS ON "CHILDREN OBEY YOUR PARENTS"

17:3-4	p 135
18:4	p 134
19	p 178
19:8	p 134
19:26	p 134
20:29-30	p 132
21:8-9	p 45
27:11	p 136

Romans

2:25-29	p 49
3:20	p 50
5:19	p 71 footnote
6:14	p 50
7:6	p 50
7:7	p 50
8:2-5	p 53
8:14-16	p 50
8:16, 17, 21	p 67
8:38	p 135
10:4	p 50
12:10	p 70
13:10	p 50
14:4	p 112

1 Corinthians

2:9-12	p 50
3:2	p 185
3:16-17	p 49
11:1	p 126

2 Corinthians

2:9	pp 124-126
3:12-16	p 49
4:6-7	p 176
5:11	p 134
11:13-15a	p 132

Galatians

3:29	p 49
5:13	p 70
5:14	p 51
5:16-18	p 53

Ephesians

1:3-4	p 175
1:17-21	p 44
2:6	p 167-168
2:11-22	p 49
2:12-13	p 49
4:2	p 70
4:11-16	p 52
4:14-15	p 144
5:1-2	pp 67-68
5:8-9	p 68
5:14	p 50
5:21	p 72
5:28-29	p 203
6	pp 76-77, 110, 203
6:1	p 61
6:1-3	p 57, 65
6:1-4	p 59
6:3	p 203
6:4	p 68
6:10-13	pp 60, 145, 170
6:10-18	p 21
6:12	p 175
6:16	p 181

Colossians

2:6-10	p 75
2:9-10	p 175
2:11-12	p 49
2:16-17	p 50

APPENDIX B: QUESTIONS ON "CHILDREN OBEY YOUR PARENTS"

3:1-3	p 58
3:13	p 70
3:18-21	p 59
3:20	pp 57, 60-65
3:21	p 68

1 Thessalonians

4:18	p 70

1 Timothy

2:5	pp 33, 74, 109
6:8	p 98

2 Timothy

1:1-2	p 202
1:2	p 201
1:5	p 135
1:12	p 135
3:1-5	p 143
4:3-4	p 133

Titus

3:9	p 50

Hebrews

2:17	p 49
3:1-6	p 51
3:5-6	p 122
3:13	pp 70, 151
4:14-16	pp 49, 181
4:16	p 74
6:9	p 135
7:4	p 5
7:26-28	p 50
8:5-7	p 51
8:6	p 48, 51
9:1-5	p 49
9:15	p 49
10:1-2	p 50

10:5-7, 12	p 50
10:11-14	p 50
10:12, 18	p 55 footnote
11:6	p 87
11:13	p 135
12:18-24	p 54
13:9	p 145
13:17	pp 129-146

James

4:6b-7	p 181
5:16	p 70

1 Peter

1:13-15	p 67
2:4-10	p 49
2:5	p 49
2:9	p 49
3:5-6	pp 201-202
3:8	p 70
5:1-3	p 140

2 Peter

1:3-4	p 56
2:1-3	p 133

1 John

3:10	p 67
3:11, 23	p 70
4:1	p 145

Revelation

5:12	p 29
12:10-11	p 178

About the Author

SINCE 2006 REBECCA DAVIS has been studying and learning about abuse and trauma, especially through the first-person accounts of many of her friends. For about thirty years longer than that, she has been an avid student of the Scriptures.

She has enjoyed teaching truth to many through the years, to groups as large as five hundred and as small as four or five, about topics as diverse as the realities of abuse, hope through the grief of Alzheimer's, miracles and gospel opportunities in the lives of missionaries, the true freedom and gracious life transformation to be found in Jesus Christ, and of course, untwisting Scriptures.

Rebecca is the author or collaborating author of 19 books for children and adults. Her adult books are written to help those who have been abused find hope in the Lord Jesus Christ, and to help Christians have a deeper understanding of the true God and His love for them. This is her desire for this book, the second in the *Untwisting Scriptures* series.

Rebecca enjoys getting together with friends, listening to their stories, and offering hope through Jesus Christ. She and her husband Tim have four adult children and a growing group of grandchildren.

You can connect with her at her websites heresthejoy.com and rebeccadaviswordworking.com.

A Note from the Author

I'M PRAYING THAT as you read, your eyes will be open to the truth of the goodness of the true God, the true Lord Jesus Christ, and His love for those who come to Him in faith.

If this book has been helpful to you, would you consider leaving a review on Amazon? Those who are searching for a helpful book will often search on Amazon even if they plan to buy the book elsewhere, because the reviews are so valuable.

Good reviews will help get this book into the hands of more people who need to have Scriptures untwisted to help them walk in spiritual freedom. You can search for the book by the title and then click on "leave a review." Thank you.

You can also go to heresthejoy.com to download your copy of my free Guide, *How to Enjoy the Bible Again after Spiritual Abuse (without feeling guilty or getting triggered out of your mind).*

Made in the USA
Monee, IL
30 May 2023

34961048R00125